Censorship Issues

ISSUES

Volume 196

Series Editor

Lisa Firth

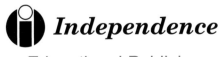

Independence

Educational Publishers

Cambridge

First published by Independence

The Studio, High Green

Great Shelford

Cambridge CB22 5EG

England

© Independence 2010

British Library Cataloguing in Publication Data

Censorship issues. -- (Issues ; v. 196)

1. Censorship.

I. Series II. Firth, Lisa.

363.3'1-dc22

ISBN-13: 978 1 86168 558 2

Printed in Great Britain

MWL Print Group Ltd

CONTENTS

Chapter 1 The Free Speech Debate

Chapter 2 Regulation and Standards

Chapter 3 Censoring the Internet

OTHER TITLES IN THE ISSUES SERIES

For more on these titles, visit: www.independence.co.uk

EXPLORING THE ISSUES

Photocopiable study guides to accompany the above publications. Each four-page A4 guide provides a variety of discussion points and other activities to suit a wide range of ability levels and interests.

A note on critical evaluation

Because the information reprinted here is from a number of different sources, readers should bear in mind the origin of the text and whether the source is likely to have a particular bias when presenting information (just as they would if undertaking their own research). It is hoped that, as you read about the many aspects of the issues explored in this book, you will critically evaluate the information presented. It is important that you decide whether you are being presented with facts or opinions. Does the writer give a biased or an unbiased report? If an opinion is being expressed, do you agree with the writer?

Censorship Issues offers a useful starting point for those who need convenient access to information about the many issues involved. However, it is only a starting point. Following each article is a URL to the relevant organisation's website, which you may wish to visit for further information.

Restrictions on press freedom intensifying

Information from Freedom House.

Global press freedom declined in 2009, with setbacks registered in almost every region of the world, according to a Freedom House study released today. The study, *Freedom of the Press 2010: A Global Survey of Media Independence*, reported that press freedom declined for the eighth consecutive year, producing a global landscape in which only one in six people live in countries with a press rated Free. Among the report's key findings:

⇨ Significant declines outnumbered gains by a 2-to-1 margin. Notable regional declines were registered in Sub-Saharan Africa and Latin America, as well as the Middle East.

⇨ Declines in important emerging democracies demonstrate the fragility of press freedom in such environments. Namibia and South Africa, two of the new democracies, dropped from Free to Partly Free. Worrying declines were also registered in Mexico, the Philippines and Senegal.

> *'Freedom of expression is fundamental to all other freedoms. Rule of law, fair elections, minority rights, freedom of association, and accountable government all depend on an independent press'*

⇨ The only region to show overall improvement was Asia-Pacific, spurred by notable gains in South Asia that included status changes in Bangladesh and Bhutan from Not Free to Partly Free and a numerical score jump for the Maldives.

⇨ Governments in China, Russia, Venezuela, and other countries have been systematically encroaching on the comparatively free environment of the Internet and new media. Sophisticated techniques are being used to censor and block access to particular types of information, to flood the Internet with antidemocratic, nationalistic views, and to provide broad surveillance of citizen activity.

⇨ Journalists are increasingly the victims of assault and murder, a trend fuelled by impunity for past crimes.

'Freedom of expression is fundamental to all other freedoms. Rule of law, fair elections, minority rights, freedom of association, and accountable government all depend on an independent press which can fulfill its watchdog function,' said Jennifer Windsor, executive director of Freedom House. 'This is why these findings are so utterly disturbing. When the Iranian Revolutionary Guards torture a journalist, or Communist authorities in China imprison a blogger, or criminal elements in Russia assassinate yet another investigative reporter, it sends a clear message that every person fighting for basic rights is vulnerable to a similar fate.'

While a range of restrictive laws and violence against journalists continue to hamper media freedom, additional reasons for the global decline include the unique pressures placed on media in countries in the midst of political conflict, as well as intensified constraints on Internet freedom. The globalisation of censorship by countries such as China and international bodies such as the Organization of the Islamic Conference poses an additional threat to freedom of expression, as does the increasingly worrisome phenomenon of 'libel tourism' centred on the United Kingdom.

30-year trends

In the 30 years since Freedom House began measuring global media freedom, the landscape has changed considerably:

⇨ In 1980, media freedom was concentrated in Western Europe; only 22 per cent of the world's countries enjoyed a rating of Free, while 53 per cent were Not Free.

⇨ By 1990, the share of Not Free countries had declined to 47 per cent; by 2000, it was just 35 per cent.

⇨ Over the past decade, the positive momentum that followed the fall of the Berlin Wall has stalled, and in some cases has been reversed. For the past eight years, there have been gradual declines on a global scale, with the most pronounced setbacks taking place in Latin America and the former Soviet Union.

FREEDOM HOUSE

'Unfortunately, the positive changes seen in earlier decades have not been consolidated,' noted Karin Deutsch Karlekar, managing editor of the study. 'While the media landscape around the world has opened considerably – due in part to the impact of privately owned and satellite broadcast media and the Internet – both governments and non-state actors have found new ways to restrict the independence of the media and the free flow of information.'

'The steps backwards taken by a number of the new democracies are particularly disturbing,' said Karlekar, citing the declines in Namibia, the Philippines, Senegal and South Africa as examples. 'Journalists in many countries cannot do their job without fear of repercussions.'

Key regional findings

The Americas:

Despite the lack of status changes during the year, overall decline in the region was apparent. The most significant declines were registered in Mexico and Honduras, which both hover on the cusp of the Not Free range. Other declines occurred in Ecuador, Nicaragua and Venezuela.

Asia-Pacific:

The Asia-Pacific region saw some of the most significant improvement observed in the study, including status changes from Not Free to Partly Free in Bangladesh and Bhutan. Improvements were also seen in the Maldives, India, East Timor, Indonesia, Papua New Guinea and Mongolia. Declines were noted in Afghanistan, Sri Lanka, Nepal, the Philippines and Fiji. This region also continues to be the home of two of the survey's poorest performers, North Korea and Burma, and the world's largest poor performer, China.

Central and Eastern Europe/former Soviet Union:

In 2009, the region overall underwent a modest decline, with most countries showing little or no change. In the non-Baltic former Soviet Union, where media freedoms are severely restricted, Russia remained among the world's more repressive and most dangerous media environments. Kyrgyzstan's score fell, continuing a multi-year negative trend. Ukraine, Armenia, and Moldova registered slight improvements. Apart from the former Soviet Union, modest declines were seen in Latvia and Lithuania, with even smaller negative movements in Estonia, Hungary and Croatia.

Middle East and North Africa:

Iran registered the region's biggest decline of the year due to the suppression of journalists in the wake of a seriously flawed presidential election. Tunisia, Algeria, Morocco and the United Arab Emirates also registered declines. Israel provided one of the few positive developments in the region, returning to Free from Partly Free status thanks to the removal of restrictions associated with the 2008 outbreak of war in the Gaza Strip, which had depressed the country's ranking in the 2009 survey. In addition, Iraq saw another year of improvement as political bias declined and attacks on journalists decreased.

Sub-Saharan Africa:

The average regionwide level of press freedom declined significantly during 2009, representing the largest overall drop of any region in the survey. Africa saw two surprising status changes, with South Africa and Namibia both dropping from Free to Partly Free, leaving no Free countries in southern Africa for the first time since 1990. Meanwhile, Madagascar shifted into the Not Free category. Declines were also registered in Senegal, Niger, Guinea, Benin, Botswana, Togo, Guinea-Bissau, Gabon, Ethiopia and The Gambia. Slight improvements were noted in Zimbabwe, Kenya, Sudan and Mauritania.

A range of restrictive laws and violence against journalists continue to hamper media freedom

Western Europe:

The region registered no status changes or significant numerical shifts in 2009, reflecting a largely steady level of media freedom in most countries. The United Kingdom remains a concern due to its expansive libel laws, while heavy media concentration and official interference in state-owned outlets continues to hold Italy at Partly Free.

Worst of the worst

The world's ten worst-rated countries are Belarus, Burma, Cuba, Equatorial Guinea, Eritrea, Iran, Libya, North Korea, Turkmenistan and Uzbekistan. In these states, independent media are either non-existent or barely able to operate, the press acts as a mouthpiece for the regime, citizens' access to unbiased information is severely limited, and dissent is crushed through imprisonment, torture and other forms of repression.

Freedom House is an independent watchdog organisation that supports democratic change, monitors the status of freedom around the world, and advocates for democracy and human rights.

29 April 2010

⇨ The above information is reprinted with kind permission from Freedom House. Visit http://freedomhouse.org for more information.

© *Freedom House*

PCC rejects Jan Moir complaint

Information from politics.co.uk

By Ian Dunt

The Press Complaints Commission (PCC) has rejected a complaint into the now-infamous article written by *Daily Mail* journalist Jan Moir into the death of Stephen Gately.

The commission received a record 25,000 complaints about the piece, which appeared to suggest that his premature death was a result of his gay lifestyle.

The commission admitted being 'uncomfortable with the tenor of the columnist's remarks' but said finding against the *Mail* would represent a 'slide towards censorship'.

'Argument and debate are working parts of an active society and should not be constrained unnecessarily,' the judgement read.

The piece became a popular trending topic on Twitter and the outraged reaction to Ms Moir's argument represented one of the first major effects of the new social networking site on mainstream debate.

But some commentators worried about a new era of censorship if the outrage expressed on Twitter changed the *Mail*'s editorial stance or forced it to remove the piece.

In the end, Ms Moir offered an apology for any pain she may have caused.

'While many complainants considered that there was an underlying tone of negativity towards Mr Gately and the complainant [Andrew Cowles, Gately's civil partner] on account of the fact that they were gay, it was not possible to identify any direct uses of pejorative or prejudicial language in the article,' the ruling said.

A distinction must be drawn 'between critical innuendo which, though perhaps distasteful, was permissible in a free society – and discriminatory description of individuals, and the code was designed to constrain the latter rather than the former,' the commission said.

18 February 2010

⇨ The above information is reprinted with kind permission from politics.co.uk

What is the PCC?

Information from Press Complaints Commission.

The Press Complaints Commission is an independent body which deals with complaints from members of the public about the editorial content of newspapers and magazines. Our service to the public is free, quick and easy. We aim to deal with most complaints in just 35 working days – and there is absolutely no cost to the people complaining.

Of the complaints received that are specified under the terms of the Code of Practice approximately two in three are about accuracy in reporting and approximately one in five relate to intrusion into privacy of some sort. All complaints are investigated under the editors' Code of Practice, which binds all national and regional newspapers and magazines. The Code – drawn up by editors themselves – covers the way in which news is gathered and reported. It also provides special protection to particularly vulnerable groups of people such as children, hospital patients and those at risk of discrimination.

Our main aim with any complaint which raises a possible breach of the Code of Practice is always to resolve it as quickly as possible. Because of our success in this, the Commission had to adjudicate on only 39 complaints in 2009. That is a sign not of the weakness of self-regulation – but its strength. All those which were critical of a newspaper were published in full and with due prominence by the publication concerned.

As well as dealing with complaints, the PCC deals with a substantial number of calls from members of the public about our service and about the Code. In 2009 we dealt with approximately 37,000 enquiries by telephone, fax and email. This is an encouraging sign of the accessibility of the Commission to members of the public.

The success of the PCC continues to underline the strength of effective and independent self regulation over any form of legal or statutory control. Legal controls would be useless to those members of the public who could not afford legal action – and would mean protracted delays before complainants received redress. In our system of self-regulation, effective redress is free and quick. An overview of the benefits of self-regulation can be found on the PCC website.

⇨ The above information is reprinted with kind permission from the Press Complaints Commission. Visit /www.pcc.org.uk for more information.

Confusing censoring with censuring

The complaints commission's ruling on Jan Moir and Stephen Gately suggests the PCC does not understand its own role.

By Emma Woollcott

Many questions may be asked about the adjudication on Jan Moir's article on Stephen Gately's death. Is it right that all opinion in print media should be protected on the basis of freedom of expression? Should 'comment' not be distinguished clearly from assertions of fact? Does there not have to be a factual basis for comment, and a genuine public interest in its publication? Would the Press Complaints Commission (PCC) have made the same decision absent of the 'orchestrated campaign' against the *Daily Mail* article? Might the adjudication have been different if the complaints about the article had related to racial or religious abuse, rather than homophobia? Can self-regulation be effective where those who regulate an industry have a commercial interest in the outcome of their decisions?

One question, however, stands out: does the PCC understand its own role and the nature of the sanctions it can impose?

The PCC's chairman, Baroness Buscombe, told Radio 4's *Today* programme that the adjudication of the complaint relating to Moir's article had been a difficult one for the PCC, but that the article had 'just failed to cross the line'. The PCC concluded that the article did not breach the code, and noted that 'to rule otherwise would be to say that newspapers were not entitled to publish certain opinions (which may be disagreeable to many) on events which are matters of public discussion'. It said that 'this would be a slide towards censorship, which the commission could not endorse'.

The PCC clearly believes it has a censorial role. Is that right?

> *Article 5 [of the PCC's code] obliges newspapers to ensure that publication is handled sensitively at a time of grief*

The preamble to the code sets out that 'all members of the press have a duty to maintain the highest professional standards. The code should set a benchmark for those ethical standards, protecting both the rights of the individual and the public's right to know'. The code continues that 'it is essential that the code be honoured not only to the letter but in the full spirit'.

If the PCC upholds a complaint (or even, say, 25,000 complaints), it expresses its disapproval at the newspaper's failure to adhere to the highest standards of professional journalism, and it requires the newspaper to publish its adjudication in a prominent position. It cannot require the newspaper to remove the article, nor can it injunct the journalist or the editor against future publication. It censures the newspaper, rather than censoring it. At the same time as publishing the PCC's reprimand, the newspaper is free to continue to publish the offending article (and similar), if it wishes to do so. In no way is the newspaper's freedom of expression suppressed or restricted. The adjudication adds to the debate, rather than taking anything away.

This week the Department for Culture, Media and Sport published its second report on press standards, libel and privacy. Among its recommendations are that the PCC should be able to impose financial penalties on publications found to have breached the code. The chairman of the committee explained that the

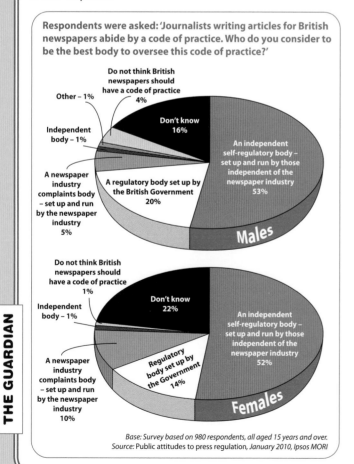

Respondents were asked: 'Journalists writing articles for British newspapers abide by a code of practice. Who do you consider to be the best body to oversee this code of practice?'

Males
- Do not think British newspapers should have a code of practice 4%
- Other – 1%
- Independent body – 1%
- Don't know 16%
- A newspaper industry complaints body – set up and run by the newspaper industry 5%
- A regulatory body set up by the British Government 20%
- An independent self-regulatory body – set up and run by those independent of the newspaper industry 53%

Females
- Do not think British newspapers should have a code of practice 1%
- Independent body – 1%
- Don't know 22%
- A newspaper industry complaints body – set up and run by the newspaper industry 10%
- Regulatory body set up by the Government 14%
- An independent self-regulatory body – set up and run by those independent of the newspaper industry 52%

Base: Survey based on 980 respondents, all aged 15 years and over.
Source: Public attitudes to press regulation, January 2010, Ipsos MORI

recommendation aimed to 'counter' the fact that the PCC is widely viewed as 'lacking credibility and authority'; that the PCC 'must be seen to be taking a more active role in ensuring that standards are upheld'. However, the power to impose financial penalties will not lend the PCC credibility if there is no confidence that it can be trusted to properly apply the code.

Can self-regulation be effective where those who regulate an industry have a commercial interest in the outcome of their decisions?

The 'slide towards censorship' quote is taken from the section of the PCC's adjudication that relates to article 5. This obliges newspapers to ensure that publication is handled sensitively at a time of grief. It is arguably the least convincing section of the PCC's deliberations.

After dismissing the inaccuracies in Moir's article on the basis that it was a 'comment' piece, based on information (and misinformation – but, they say, how was she to know?) already in the public domain, the PCC considered the effect of its publication on Andrew Cowles, Gately's civil partner. The PCC considered that 'the context of its publication was paramount'. The article had been published six days after Gately's death, on the day of the funeral. The PCC relied on the fact that Moir's views were regularly 'provocative'; that Gately 'was a famous individual in a successful pop group', whose 'life had attracted a large degree of public and media attention, as did his death'; and that this was 'not a news item, reporting on the fact of the

death, nor did it seek to provide new information about what had happened'.

No, indeed, it contained nothing new, except Moir's assertion that the result of the postmortem must be wrong – that his death could not have been from natural causes. She argued that there had been a huge cover-up – there is 'something terribly wrong in the way this incident has been shaped and spun' and 'the sugar coating on this fatality is so saccharine-thick that it obscures whatever bitter truth lies beneath'.

This is where the intrusion lies: not in how widely the fact of Gately's death had been reported in the six days since his death, but in Moir's vehement but baseless determination to argue that his partner's death must in some way have been a result of his 'lifestyle' or the 'sleazy' circumstances. Cowles' distress at the article was exacerbated by its 'underlying tone of negativity', which he and others viewed simply as homophobia. He explained to the PCC how the fact that the article had offended so many of his and Gately's friends, gay and straight, had distressed him greatly, and had been an unwelcome distraction on the day that he flew his partner's body back to Ireland for the funeral.

A predictable outcome? Probably. Sensitive publication at a time of grief? The *Daily Mail*'s Irish editor did not think so, which is why, out of respect for Stephen's family in Ireland, he did not include Moir's piece in the Irish edition.

⇨ Emma Woollcott acts for Andrew Cowles in relation to various matters, including his complaint to the PCC about the Jan Moir article.

28 February 2010

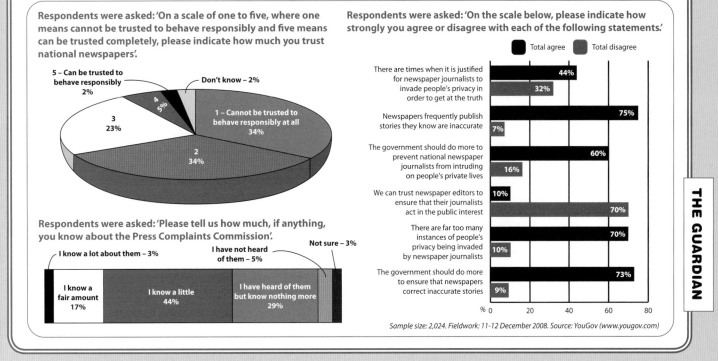

Respondents were asked: 'On a scale of one to five, where one means cannot be trusted to behave responsibly and five means can be trusted completely, please indicate how much you trust national newspapers'.

- 5 – Can be trusted to behave responsibly 2%
- 4 5%
- Don't know – 2%
- 1 – Cannot be trusted to behave responsibly at all 34%
- 2 34%
- 3 23%

Respondents were asked: 'Please tell us how much, if anything, you know about the Press Complaints Commission'.

- I know a lot about them – 3%
- I have not heard of them – 5%
- Not sure – 3%
- I know a fair amount 17%
- I know a little 44%
- I have heard of them but know nothing more 29%

Respondents were asked: 'On the scale below, please indicate how strongly you agree or disagree with each of the following statements.'

■ Total agree   ■ Total disagree

Statement	Total agree	Total disagree
There are times when it is justified for newspaper journalists to invade people's privacy in order to get at the truth	44%	32%
Newspapers frequently publish stories they know are inaccurate	75%	7%
The government should do more to prevent national newspaper journalists from intruding on people's private lives	60%	16%
We can trust newspaper editors to ensure that their journalists act in the public interest	10%	70%
There are far too many instances of people's privacy being invaded by newspaper journalists	70%	10%
The government should do more to ensure that newspapers correct inaccurate stories	73%	9%

% 0   20   40   60   80

Sample size: 2,024. Fieldwork: 11-12 December 2008. Source: YouGov (www.yougov.com)

THE GUARDIAN

The public and press self-regulation

⇨ **An independent self-regulator not a newspaper complaints body** 52% of the public want the press regulated by an independent self-regulatory body vs only 8% who want a newspaper industry complaints body – as now.

⇨ **Monitoring and investigation more important than mediation** 73% of people think the chief purpose of this body should be to monitor compliance with the code of practice and conduct investigations where there is public concern vs 12% who believe it should be to mediate complaints between newspapers and complainants – as now.

⇨ **An obligation to investigate, not wait for complaint** Almost half (48%) of the public think this body should be obligated to investigate where there is evidence of inaccuracy in newspapers vs 5% who think it should wait for a complaint from someone directly referred to in an article – as now.

⇨ **Limited support for government regulation of the press** Only 17% of the public were in favour of a government regulator vs 52% who wanted an independent self-regulatory body.

⇨ **Self-regulation should represent the interest of the general public as well as the complainant** 61% of people thought it was 'very important' that an independent press self-regulatory body represented the interests of the general public, while 57% thought it very important it represent the interests of the complainant.

⇨ **Public support for financial penalties** 85% of the public think it would be appropriate to impose fines on newspapers, in serious cases.

⇨ **Strong public backing for greater transparency** 79% think it important that the minutes of PCC meetings be made public.

75% think it should be clear who funds press self-regulation and 69% believe the amount each funder contributes should be made public.

21 January 2010

⇨ The above information is an extract from the Media Standards Trust press release *Strong public support for reform of press self-regulation* and is reprinted with permission. See www.mediastandardstrust.org for more.

© *Media Standards Trust*

PCC attitude survey

The PCC undertook a comprehensive polling exercise with Toluna – the world's largest independent online panel and survey technology provider to the global market research industry – to measure public attitudes towards the PCC and self-regulation of the press, from a nationally representative sample of 1,017 adults.

This study is part of a regular measurement of public attitudes. It demonstrated strong approval of the present structures, activity and sanctions of the PCC system but some scope for improving the depth of knowledge of public awareness of the PCC.

The results showed:

⇨ **Awareness** 81% of people were aware of the PCC.

⇨ **Proactivity** 58% think it would be improper for the PCC to publicise their views on a case before consent or solicitation. Only 25% thought it would be proper. This suggests that the notion that the PCC should take all third party complaints, or issue public warnings of their own volition, does not have public support.

⇨ **Monitoring** Twice as many people believe the PCC should respond to complaints when they arise rather than try to monitor every article which appears.

⇨ **Effectiveness** Only 14% of the public thought that the PCC was ineffective.

⇨ **Commission composition** 51% think the Commission should be a mixture of public and senior journalists (significantly outscoring all other options by four times).

⇨ **Code of Practice** Two-thirds of the population agree that the current solution for applying and amending the Code is proper (only 7% thought not proper). This shows clear support for the system of editors being responsible for the Code, and the PCC for enforcing it.

⇨ **Fine vs apology** Three-quarters of the population (77%) prefer a quick public apology to a lengthy process and fine.

⇨ **Funding** Almost nine out of ten people believe the PCC system should be funded by the newspaper and magazine industry (rather than taxpayer, complainants).

April 2010

⇨ The above information is reprinted with kind permission from the Press Complaints Commission (PCC). Full results of this polling can be found at www.pcc.org.uk/assets/111/PCC_Survey_2010.pdf

© *PCC*

MEDIA STANDARDS TRUST / PRESS COMPLAINTS COMMISSION

The BNP: no platform, no exceptions

Information from LabourList.org

By Ellie Levenson

I posted a message on Twitter recently, in the midst of discussions in the news about whether Labour would put people forward to share a platform with the BNP. My message was simple. It said: 'For the record, I would not share a platform, *Question Time* or other, with BNP representative.' One of the responses I got was from a Conservative Party member who lives in the same constituency as me. His response: 'would they share one with YOU?' (his capitals not mine). And you know what, I suspect they wouldn't. Because I am Jewish.

There is a very simple reason why no other political party should share a platform with the BNP. That is because they are racist. We can make other arguments too, including arguments about lies and intimidation – but that they are racist should be enough.

When we argue against other mainstream parties we disagree on points of policy and on ideology. They might want us to have a different type of relationship to the state, different levels of access to public services, different types of education or even different types of relationships. But they do not wish some of us to be second-class citizens, exiled or worse based on our ethnicity. Whatever we think of the individual policies of other mainstream parties, their policies are not racist policies. That is why our system works, because to take part in it all parties have to sign up to some basic moral tenets. The BNP does not do this.

If the Labour Government, and other mainstream political parties, share a platform with the BNP they give the message that the BNP has policies you should listen to and think about and then decide whether to give them your support. What they should be doing is saying supporting the BNP should not be an option, because whatever the non-racist policies they have are, whether you like the sound of their ideas about tax or justice or health (and some of their policies on this can come across as attractive), the very fact the party has racist policies at its core is enough that we should deny them the right to discuss anything else.

This alone should stop any decent politicians from any party sharing a platform with the BNP. But more than that; if we did share a platform who would we ask to do this? Whoever we choose there is a problem. Either we choose someone from one of the groups the BNP hate – neither appropriate or fair. Or we choose someone from the one group that the BNP do not hate – someone white and ethnically British, whatever that may be. And we end up with a platform that looks just how the BNP would like the country to look.

Both scenarios disgust me and they should disgust every member of every mainstream party. That is why Tom Flynn, an anti-BNP campaigner and Labour PPC for Southend West, and I have set up a Facebook group 'BNP – No Platform. No Exceptions'. We want supporters of all parties to join and for MPs, Councillors, journalists, commentators, campaigners and anyone who might ever be asked to share a platform with the BNP to publicly give their support to the group. Because if we all refuse to share a platform then we show the BNP to be the marginal party that it is.

Ellie Levenson is a freelance journalist and a member of Tottenham CLP.

21 September 2009

⇨ This article first appeared at LabourList.org

Why 'no platform' is incompatible with freedom of speech

The refusal by mainstream parties to debate with the BNP is illiberal and reactionary, argues Suzy Dean. It demeans us, the public, and the democratic election process.

By Suzy Dean

So far freedom has failed to become a hot issue in the general election despite numerous curtailments to individual and collective liberties over the past five years, from anti-terror laws to the ban on smoking in pubs. In fact, the election itself is appearing to damage another one of our most fundamental freedoms, our freedom of speech. As the election draws closer and debate heats up, both Conservative and Labour candidates have started to refuse to debate the BNP. This is something that we should all challenge as it demeans us – the public – and our democratic election process.

In Chippenham last week both Labour and Conservative candidates refused to take part in a debate if Michael Simpkins, the BNP candidate for the local area, was present. On Sunday, the Archbishop of Canterbury backed a decision to ban the BNP from election hustings in a Lancashire church. The assumption seems to be that if we are allowed to see and hear the BNP, we will listen and agree. But in fact, the majority of us do not, and will not, constitute a racist mob. Anybody should be able to run with their views in an election, whatever they are, in a bid to canvass some support. It is then down to us to decide if we want to give them our vote.

Not allowing the BNP to debate shows serious contempt for the public's political judgement. Chippenham Tory opposition, Wilfred Emmanuel-Jones, called the BNP 'disgusting' and 'racist'. The local Labour candidate Greg Lovell admitted that the BNP 'don't have an enormous presence'. Both of these comments are true, which is why the BNP have never had more than a handful of supporters. So why don't we let them hang themselves in the court of public debate? Why has refusing to debate the BNP become the thing to do?

Superiority

No platform for the BNP is a crude attempt to show moral and political superiority of the mainstream parties over the BNP. But the BNP do not just represent themselves, they represent a section of the public. Refusing to debate the BNP is refusing to acknowledge ideas that a part, albeit a minority, of our society holds to be the right ones. The reality is that the BNP's arguments are legitimate if they have enough support to run for election. Griffin's support cannot just be filtered out, it needs to be taken up, picked apart and contested through public debate. For politicians to simply censor the BNP is to say that they don't believe in democracy and their own powers of persuasion – they don't believe they need to win the argument.

> ## The foundation of our democracy is the idea that individuals are capable of moral and political reasoning

The foundation of our democracy is the idea that individuals are capable of moral and political reasoning. It is sad that Simpkins had to be the one to argue that if the public don't like what the BNP have to say 'they can show their disgust for me at the ballot box by voting for somebody else'. It is uncomfortable to think that mainstream parties are being illiberal and reactionary when they challenge the idea of civic rationality and the BNP aren't.

The implication of banning the BNP is that they remain part of political discourse when they should be politically mauled and tossed to one side. Mainstream politicians should move beyond the hype and have confidence that they can win a debate against Griffin and Co. If anything, mainstream politicians and activists should be encouraging the BNP to have more public debates in an attempt to diminish their already measly support base even further.

Suzy Dean is a writer and journalist and co-founder of To The Point manifesto.

28 April 2010

THE FREE SOCIETY

British troops harassed by anti-war protesters during homecoming parade

Muslim extremists were put on trial after publicly declaring that British soldiers are 'baby killers and rapists'.

By Carolyn Kirby

Seven Muslim men were brought to trial for abusive behaviour towards homecoming troops in Luton town centre. Having recently returned from a tour of duty, 200 servicemen and women marched through the streets of the Bedfordshire town in March 2009, and the parade was attended by many locals wishing to show their support. But the group of Muslim extremists used the ceremonial parade as a chance to demonstrate their opposition to the wars in Iraq and Afghanistan, shouting abuse at members of the 2nd Battalion of the Royal Anglian Regiment.

At the trial in January 2010, the Luton Magistrates Court heard how the Muslim men had shouted phrases such as 'Baby killers and rapists, all of you', 'Burn in hell' and 'British soldiers, murderers', whilst bearing placards that read 'Butchers of Basra'. Members of the public who lined the streets to show their support for the soldiers were clearly upset and distressed by the disruptive behaviour.

An anti-war protest had been previously arranged with the local police, and a designated protest site was set up in the town centre. However, the demonstration got out of hand, resulting in police attempting to control the offensive behaviour directed at the British troops.

Jalal Ahmed, 21, Yousaf Bashir, 29, Ziaur Rahman, 32, Shajjadar Choudhury, 31, Munim Abdul, 28, Ibrahim Anderson, 32, and Jubair Ahmed, 19, were charged with a breach of Section 5 of the Public Order Act, which states that it is a criminal offence to cause disturbance in a public area or shout abuse at members of the public. During the trial the defendants, who all live in Luton, refused to stand for the Judge, disregarding conventional courtroom protocol.

The defence lawyers argued that the case was a matter of freedom of speech, and one lawyer even cited the famous quote often attributed to Voltaire: 'I disagree with what you say but I will defend to the death your right to say it', asserting that even if members of the community did not like what they heard, they should accept that everyone has a right to freedom of expression. However, the prosecutor, Avirup Chaudhuri, disputed this, claiming that the slogans used by the Islamic extremists 'fell within the category of threatening, abusive and insulting words and behaviour' and that the language used 'goes beyond legitimate protests'.

A spokesman from the 2nd Battalion, who are commonly known as 'The Poachers', said that they had been 'deeply touched' by the support shown by the public. The high attendance level by the local community was also commented on by Inspector James Goldsmith as he addressed the Magistrates Court.

After a five-day trial, District Judge Carolyn Mellanby convicted five out of the seven men for abusive behaviour. Although all seven defendants pleaded not guilty, only two were cleared of all charges. The verdict came after Judge Carolyn Mellanby stated that: 'Citizens of Luton are entitled to demonstrate their support for the troops without experiencing insults and abuse...[the defendants] were fully aware that shocking phrases in such circumstances would inevitably cause distress'. The five defendants who were found guilty of the charges were sentenced with two-year conditional discharges and ordered to pay £500 each.

17 August 2010

INDEPENDENCE

The Luton protesters should not have been convicted

Fight bigots with rational argument, not repression.

By Peter Tatchell

Yesterday, five Muslim men who protested at a homecoming parade by soldiers from the Royal Anglian Regiment in Luton in March 2009 were convicted under the Public Order Act.

The conviction of these five men, for using threatening, abusive or insulting words or behaviour likely to cause harassment, alarm or distress, is a dangerous infringement of free speech and the right to protest. I abhor everything they stand for, but defend their right to freedom of expression. Even though what they said was offensive to many people, their right to speak their mind is one of the hallmarks of a democratic society.

They want to destroy our democracy and freedoms. I want to defend these values. If we silence and criminalise their views, we are little better than them. As the judge in the case, Carolyn Mellanby was wrong to rule that the people of Luton have a right to be protected against words they find insulting. There is no right not to be offended, as almost any idea can be offensive to someone. Many of the greatest thinkers in history have caused insult and offence, including Galileo Galilei and Charles Darwin.

The five convicted Islamists would like to censor us and put us on trial. We should not stoop to their level of intolerance. Democracy is superior to their proposed theocratic state and we need to prove it by demonstrating that we allow objectionable opinions and contest them by debate, not by repression and censorship.

I strongly disagree with these men and their fundamentalist religion. They seek to establish an Islamist dictatorship in the UK. I reject the hatred and religious tyranny they espouse. They oppose women's rights, gay equality, people of other faiths and Muslims who do not conform to their hardline interpretation of Islam.

But I defend their right to express their opinions, even though they are offensive and distressing to many people.

Insult and offence are not sufficient grounds, in a democratic society, to criminalise words and actions. The criminalisation of insulting, abusive or offensive speech is wrong. The only words that should be criminalised are untrue defamations and threats of violence, such as falsely branding someone as a paedophile, or inciting murder.

Some sections of the Public Order Act inhibit the right to free speech and the right to protest. They should be repealed.

Just as I defended the right to free speech of the Christian homophobe Harry Hammond, and opposed his conviction in 2002 for insulting the gay community, so I defend the right of these Muslim fundamentalists to make their views heard, provided they don't incite violence. The best way to respond to such fanatics is to expose and refute their hateful, bigoted opinions.

Rational argument is more effective and ethical than using an authoritarian law to censor and suppress them.

Peter Tatchell is a human rights campaigner: petertatchell. net

12 January 2010

⇨ The above information is reprinted with kind permission from the *New Statesman*. Visit www. newstatesman.com for more information.

FUNNILY ENOUGH, I DEFEND YOUR RIGHTS TO UTTER A LOT OF WRONGS!

NEW STATESMAN

Atheists and ASBOs: what price offence?

The conviction of Liverpool atheist Harry Taylor for placing 'offensive' cartoons in an airport prayer room has caused controversy among secularists. Butterflies and Wheels' Ophelia Benson and Paul Sims of New Humanist magazine go head to head.

Ophelia Benson: the right to believe doesn't mean the right not to be offended

Harry Taylor left some cartoons or leaflets in a 'prayer room' at a municipal airport, and for this non-crime he was convicted of 'causing religiously aggravated harassment, alarm or distress'. He was sentenced to six months in jail suspended for two years, 100 hours of unpaid work, £250 in court costs, and an anti-social behaviour order banning him from carrying religiously offensive material in a public place.

To me this sounds like a thought experiment or a joke intended to illustrate what happens when people get so neurotically obsessed with 'communities' and 'identity' and 'faith' and 'respect' that they lose all sense of the difference between mere offence and real harm.

It is not difficult to see why some people would find what Taylor did 'offensive'; it is even possible to see why they might find it very, very, very, offensive. But the problem there is that no matter how many 'verys' you add to 'offensive', you still don't get a crime.

Lots of things are offensive. On grumpy days it can seem that the world consists largely of offensive sights, sounds, smells, behaviours, people, songs, movies, TV shows, political views – you name it. But that is too bad. We just have to put up with it. We don't get to declare everything we dislike a crime, and we don't get to send everybody who annoys us to jail.

That is, we shouldn't get to do that, but in certain circumstances, it turns out, we do. Given the right combination of sentimental protectiveness toward 'faith' and half-frightened deference to 'communities' we get to do exactly that. The *Liverpool Daily Post* reported Nicky Lees, the airport chaplain (and since when do airports have chaplains?), as saying:

'I was insulted, deeply offended and I was alarmed. I was so concerned that I rang the duty manager and the airport police. I was alarmed other people could come in and see these items and also feel offended and affronted and I was responsible for the prayer room.'

She was insulted, deeply offended, alarmed, and so concerned that she called the police. That's the problem right there: being offended, even deeply offended, should not be a reason to call the police. The reason for that is simple and obvious enough: if being deeply offended is sufficient reason to call the police and charge the offender with a crime and punish the offender with a harsh sentence, then soon there will be nothing left. Nothing at all. No books, no TV, no magazines, no Internet, no conversation; nothing. Putting up with being offended is the price we pay for having ideas.

Ophelia Benson is editor of the website Butterflies and Wheels

Paul Sims: Atheists should choose their free speech battles

No religion or belief system should receive special protection from criticism, ridicule or even insult. But at the same time individual adherents of any religion or belief system should be free to practise their belief without obstruction or harassment from those that disagree with them. Sometimes these core secular values will come into conflict, and when they do we need to pay particular attention to the context and detail of the given case, rather than reach for the blunt instrument of absolute rights. This is why I disagree with many of my fellow secularists over the conviction for 'causing religiously aggravated harassment, alarm or distress' of Harry Taylor, the 59-year-old atheist who left cartoons mocking various religions in the prayer room of Liverpool John Lennon Airport.

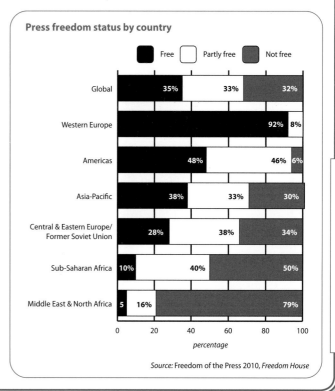

Press freedom status by country

Legend: ■ Free □ Partly free ▨ Not free

Region	Free	Partly free	Not free
Global	35%	33%	32%
Western Europe	92%		8%
Americas	48%	46%	6%
Asia-Pacific	38%	33%	30%
Central & Eastern Europe/Former Soviet Union	28%	38%	34%
Sub-Saharan Africa	10%	40%	50%
Middle East & North Africa	5	16%	79%

percentage (0 – 20 – 40 – 60 – 80 – 100)

Source: Freedom of the Press 2010, Freedom House

Taylor, who was convicted on 23 April, received a suspended prison sentence of six months, 100 hours of community service, £250 costs, and a five-year ASBO for his troubles. Secularists fell over themselves to denounce the verdict, arguing it represented a draconian attack on free speech and, in the words of Terry Sanderson of the National Secular Society, the introduction of 'a blasphemy law that covers all religions and is much more powerful than the one that was abolished only two years ago'. By this view, the case provides yet more evidence of how our society caves in to religious over-sensitivity.

But let's consider for a moment exactly what Taylor did. On three occasions between November and December 2008, he walked into the prayer room at Liverpool Airport and left posters featuring cartoons mocking religion. He was nothing if not an equal-opportunities offender – one cartoon showed a woman kneeling in front of a priest, another had Jesus stuck to the cross with no-more-nails glue and another showed a pig excreting sausages labelled 'Qu'ran'. On the third occasion the airport chaplain found the cartoons and alerted the police – in court in March, she said she was 'insulted', 'deeply offended' and 'alarmed other people could come in and see these items'.

So who is the victim here, whose rights have been violated? On the one hand we have Harry Taylor's right to subject religion to criticism and ridicule, on the other the prayer room users' rights to practise their beliefs free from harassment. Taylor has been convicted of violating the latter, and secularists must ask themselves whether he should have been allowed to do so in order to protect his own right to criticise religion.

In my view the context matters a great deal. If Taylor had been convicted for publishing the images in a magazine, or on a website, where members of the public have the choice not to buy or visit, I would strongly oppose his conviction. But this isn't what Taylor did – he placed the images in a room provided for the religious to quietly practise their faith, away from public space. He did this several times and deliberately. Why did he do it? He claims that it was a protest about the very existence of a prayer room in an airport named after John Lennon (the man who penned the line 'Imagine there's no heaven'), and a way of expressing his own religion of 'reason and rationality'. But is this reasonable? If his aim was to protest the prayer room, and not about offence at all, surely the 'rational' way to do this is to take it up with the airport authorities, write a letter to the media or stage a protest as is his right. But given the confrontational nature of the material, isn't it entirely plausible that his aim was in fact to 'harass, alarm or distress' religious believers by making them feel uncomfortable using a room provided precisely to allow them to feel comfortable practising their faith in a busy public building? And it follows that the chaplain was right to inform the police once she discovered that someone who clearly had no business in the prayer room was leaving this material in public view with a deliberateness that certainly warranted investigation.

For some secular commentators, the airport chaplain is emblematic of the trend towards crying foul at the merest slight to religious sensibilities. Is this fair? The chaplain, when she reported it, didn't even know then what we know now, that this was the third time Taylor had done it, and that he had significant previous – in 2006 he was convicted for leaving similar leaflets in two Manchester churches, and reportedly he caused a furore in a Tesco by unplugging their sound system because he objected to the Christmas-themed music. Much as we might want to applaud someone for cutting off the carols in the supermarket, or being brave enough to challenge Islam, Taylor's track record and unusual persistence surely marks him out as someone who poses a potential threat to users of the prayer room, the safety and comfort of whom is the chaplain's responsibility.

It wasn't the chaplain's decision to press charges against Taylor – presumably that decision was taken after the police investigated and discovered his form. What then should they have done? Overlook it on free-speech grounds, or prosecute as a way to try and stop his inappropriate free-speech grandstanding?

There is plenty wrong with Taylor's sentence. The terms of his ASBO, for example, ban him from carrying 'religiously offensive material' and it is entirely unclear what this might mean (could Taylor be nicked for walking round with a copy of *The God Delusion*, or *New Humanist* magazine under his arm?). It is regrettable that the case couldn't be dealt with without recourse to the law, but by deliberately and repeatedly targeting users of a prayer room, who have basic rights to go about their business unharried, I think it can be argued that he crossed the line between free speech and harassment. In this case, as with other self-styled provocateurs like Geert Wilders, I think we need a well-informed sense of proportion, not because I think religious rights trump free speech, but precisely the opposite. I think we need to keep our powder dry so we are ready to fight the real struggles ahead, the genuine threats to free and public speech – attempts to smuggle the blasphemy law in by the back door and the use of libel and other legal means to silence the inconvenient truth. Making Harry Taylor a martyr will be no help with this.

Paul Sims is News Editor of New Humanist *magazine.*
28 April 2010

⇨ The above information is reprinted with kind permission from Index on Censorship. Visit www.indexoncensorship.org for more information.

© *Index on Censorship*

Censorship and regulation

How film and video content is regulated in the UK.

It is perhaps a tribute (though a backhanded one) to the power of the moving image that it should be subject to far greater censorship than any other artistic medium. Current technology makes it effectively impossible to censor the written word, theatre censorship was abolished in 1968, and there has never been any systematic regulation of other art forms – anyone seeking to clamp down on such events must mount a private prosecution, a lengthy and expensive process.

However, film and video releases in Britain are amongst the most tightly-regulated in the Western world. With only a few exceptions, every commercially-released film both in cinemas and on video will have been vetted by the British Board of Film Classification (originally founded in 1912 as the British Board of Film Censors), which applies age-restrictive classifications and, in some cases, recommends cutting or otherwise altering the film in order to conform to their guidelines.

These guidelines are based on two main factors: legal requirements (for instance, unsimulated animal cruelty, indecent images of children) and the BBFC's own policies. The latter have changed enormously over the last century, ranging from rigidly applied lists of forbidden topics to the current context-based system where artistic merit is a key factor in assessing individual films.

Though this approach has undoubtedly led to a number of important films being passed either uncut or with a milder age restriction than one would expect, it is also controversial, due to the inevitable inconsistency. Some films are treated much more leniently than others with very similar content, as a result of largely subjective judgements by a handful of people.

Contrary to popular belief, the BBFC is not a government organisation. In fact, central government has no direct involvement in film censorship beyond passing legislation affecting the BBFC's activities. Local authorities have considerably more power, including the final say in whether or not certain films can be shown, though in the vast majority of cases they are happy to accept the BBFC's verdict. Indeed, this is why the BBFC was created by the film industry in the first place.

The history of British film censorship is as much social as cultural: the reasons films were banned in the 1920s (revolutionary politics) and 1950s (nudity) say as much about the society of the time as anything in the films. It is also revealing that in an era of far greater equality the BBFC is noticeably tougher on sexual violence today than it was 30 years ago, though correspondingly much more relaxed about most other issues.

As technology develops, the BBFC's role may well become less and less significant. A side-effect of its stated commitment to greater openness is that it is now easy to find out if films have been cut in their British versions and current technology makes it equally simple to order uncut and unclassified videos and DVDs from elsewhere (such material cannot be legally sold within the UK, but there are no barriers to importation). If this practice becomes widespread enough to affect the British film industry economically, it is likely that pressure will be applied on the BBFC to reflect this.

⇨ The above text is reprinted with kind permission from BFI Screenonline. Visit www.screenonline.org.uk for more information.

© BFI Screenonline

concerns may underpin the finding that whilst over three-quarters of recent film viewers 'always' or 'usually' agree with '12A' or '15' classification, this is lower than for the other categories. Although parents accept that young teenagers often enjoy scary films, there is a concern that very frequent or sustained tension or horror may be unpalatable for this age group.

Respondents in the focus groups were asked what the BBFC should look at when classifying film and it was interesting to see how closely these answers correlated with the Guidelines' key classification areas. Upon further discussion and analysis, the Guidelines were thought to mirror public attitudes on the traditional areas – language, violence, sex, drugs and imitable technique. Recommendations about tightening the link between the public and examiner response revolved around issues of execution, for example language and how best to express the ideas. Overall, the Guidelines were thought to be reflective of public attitudes.

Whilst the Guidelines currently include issues such as tone and racism/bigotry, respondents felt that these areas needed to be flagged and discussed in a more overt way. The subtleties of tone could transcend more traditional classification areas such as violence or horror and, given its potential impact on the viewing experience, was thought to demand a separate heading.

Likewise the Guidelines needed to acknowledge that violence was not always mitigated by fantasy and that realism within fantasy could be a problem for a younger audience. Highlighting the differences between visual and verbal references was thought to be another important area and something that the Guidelines needed to acknowledge. A sexual or sadistic dimension to violence was thought to increase its impact and also needed to be taken into account when classifying film.

Respondents were adept at highlighting the key classification issues and discussing their concerns; however, they also recognised the importance of both context and frequency. The use of the very strongest language at '15' was a concern and the word 'c**t' provoked an almost visceral response, with many arguing that it was unacceptable at any category. However, respondents understood that much depended on context and frequency and a 'throw away', non-directional, one-off use of the word was thought to be acceptable at '15'. Likewise there was an acceptance of clear images of real sex at '18' in non-porn works, provided that they were justified by context.

Smoking was never spontaneously raised as a classification issue and when prompted, there was no support for raising classifications on this basis.

Many respondents talked about the occasional dissonance in mood and tone between a trailer and feature film and how seeing a trailer for a horror film

before a romance – even at the same classification – could be both unexpected and unwanted. There was a great deal of support for making more cautious decisions on adverts and trailers, but a willingness to accept potentially more shocking content (within limits) in charity or public information adverts where the message needed to create impact and cut through.

Video games were also covered by the research. Some 73% of gamers agreed with the BBFC classification of games played recently and of those who disagree, the main complaint – by a margin of four to one – was that the classification was too high rather than too low.

23 June 2009

⇨ The above information is an extract from the BBFC's report *Public Opinion and the BBFC Guidelines 2009*, and is reprinted with permission. Visit www.bbfc.co.uk for more information.

© *BBFC*

BRITISH BOARD OF FILM CLASSIFICATION

The age-rating system for video games

Know what you buy. Know what you play.

The combination of the PEGI age label and content descriptors helps parents and those purchasing video games to ensure that the game they buy is appropriate for the age of the player.

How can I see if a game is suitable for my child?

The age rating of the game is shown on the front and back of the box. Do not hesitate to ask for the advice of retailers who are qualified to give information on PEGI. This way, you can be sure that the video game your child will be playing is age appropriate.

Who rates the games?

Game ratings are assigned by NICAM, an independent European institute specialised in rating content. As the PEGI administrator, they check each video game and grant a licence that allows the publisher to display the age label and specific content descriptors on the game packaging.

Each player can find the game that suits them best

Video games are one of the top leisure activities in Europe. Even though there are as many adults as children playing games today, prior knowledge of a game's content is vital. While most games (50%) are suitable for players of all ages (rated 3), there are many that are only suitable for older children and young teenagers. A smaller portion of games (5%) are specifically made for adults only (rated 18).

The video games industry has long been committed to age ratings. The PEGI system was launched in 2003 and its efficiency is based on its ability to provide the consumer at the time of purchase with appropriate advice. The rating considers the nature of the content and age suitability according to criteria developed and assessed by experts.

PEGI is used and recognised throughout Europe – PEGI-rated products are marketed in more than 30 countries today – and has the enthusiastic support of the European Commission. It is considered as a model of European harmonisation in the field of the protection of children.

PEGI Online

The development of online video games presents gamers with new possibilities. PEGI Online is an addition to the PEGI age-rating system to ensure the protection of minors in an online gaming environment and to provide information about online games.

Websites displaying the PEGI Online logo are committed to respecting the requirements set out in the PEGI Online Safety Code:

⇨ To keep the website free of all illegal and offensive content created by users.

⇨ To remove all undesirable links.

⇨ To provide appropriate reporting mechanisms.

⇨ To provide a coherent privacy policy.

⇨ The above information is reprinted with kind permission from PEGI (Pan European Game Information). Visit www.pegi.info or www.pegionline.eu for more.

© PEGI

Two levels of information to guide you

An icon that indicates the minimum recommended age

IMPORTANT: The PEGI rating considers the age suitability of a game's content, not the level of difficulty.

3 www.pegi.info **7** www.pegi.info **12** www.pegi.info **16** www.pegi.info **18** www.pegi.info

A series of game content descriptors

These icons are displayed on the back of the game box and indicate, where required, the nature of the content. There are eight icons, depending on the type of content.

VIOLENCE – Game contains depictions of violence

BAD LANGUAGE – Game contains bad language

FEAR – Game may be frightening or scary for young children

SEX – Game depicts nudity and/or sexual behaviour or sexual references

GAMBLING – Games that encourage or teach gambling

DRUGS – Game refers to, or depicts, the use of drugs*

ONLINE – Game can be played online

DISCRIMINATION – Game contains depictions of, or material which may encourage, discrimination

*includes alcohol and tobacco

PEGI

Ofcom

By its charter, the British Broadcasting Corporation (BBC) is intended and expected to censor the programmes it transmits. However, the BBC is regulated in part by the Office of Communications (Ofcom).

Ofcom is the regulator for the UK communications industries, replacing the Broadcasting Standards Commission (BSC), the Independent Television Commission (ITC), Office of Telecommunications (Oftel), the Radio Authority and the Radiocommunications Agency. It has responsibilities across television, radio, telecommunications and wireless communications services. Ofcom's principal duties are to further the interests of citizens in relation to communications matters and the interests of consumers in relevant markets where appropriate by promoting competition. Ofcom's specific duties include applying adequate protection for audiences against offensive or harmful material and unfair treatment or the infringement of privacy. From December 2003 Ofcom assumed the regulatory role of the BSC, ITC, Oftel and the Radio Authority (collectively termed the 'legacy regulators').

Unlike newspapers, which can openly propagate their own views, the television companies cannot editorialise on matters – other than broadcasting issues – which are politically or industrially controversial or relate to current public policy

Ofcom can impose the following sanctions: it can direct a broadcaster not to repeat a programme or advertisement; direct a broadcaster to publish a correction or adjudication ('lesser sanctions'); or it can fine a broadcaster; and shorten or revoke a licence (excluding the BBC, Channel 4 or S4C) ('greater sanctions'). These powers to penalise licensees and ultimately to revoke licences mean that Ofcom wields considerable influence.

Until it completes its process of consultation, Ofcom has adopted the Code of Practice published by the ITC. The ITC Programme Code sets out the editorial standards which audiences are entitled to expect from commercial television services in the UK. This requires that commercial television programmes do not offend against good taste or decency and are not likely to encourage crime or lead to disorder; that news is presented with due accuracy and impartiality, and that

due impartiality is preserved with regard to matters of political or industrial controversy or related to current public policy. The BSC fairness and privacy code of guidance and the BSC standards code of guidance also represent Ofcom's current policy.

It is a criminal offence to broadcast without a licence and the prosecution does not need to prove an intent to do so. Therefore, pirate radio stations have to keep one step ahead of the Department of Trade Inspectors, who can forfeit equipment as well as prosecute for infringements.

The Government has a power to direct that certain matters should not be broadcast on both commercial television and on the BBC. It used this power in 1988 to ban spoken comment by or in support of Sinn Fein, the Ulster UDA or any of the organisations proscribed under

earlier anti-terrorism laws. A challenge to the gagging order by the National Union of Journalists (NUJ), on the basis that it infringed the right of freedom of expression in Article 10 of the Convention, failed in the House of Lords and the application was rejected by the European Commission of Human Rights.

In 1993 the Government exercised its power to control what is broadcast by proscribing the Red Hot satellite channel, a carrier of pornographic material. This was upheld after an initial legal challenge, although there may have been an infringement of EU broadcasting law. The Government even retains the power to send in troops to take control of the BBC in the name of the Crown in extreme circumstances.

Ofcom's principal duties are to further the interests of citizens in relation to communications matters and the interests of consumers in relevant markets where appropriate by promoting competition

Unlike newspapers, which can openly propagate their own views, the television companies cannot editorialise on matters – other than broadcasting issues – which are politically or industrially controversial or relate to current public policy. Subliminal messages are prohibited and religious broadcasting is specifically controlled.

In a 2003 case before the House of Lords, the ProLife Alliance (a political party opposed to abortion and euthanasia) challenged the BBC's decision not to show its party political broadcast, which featured disturbing images of aborted foetuses. Both the BBC and independent broadcasters are subject to a duty not to show programmes that are likely to offend public feeling, but the Alliance argued that its rights under Article 10 of the Convention should outweigh such concerns. However, the House of Lords upheld the BBC's judgement of what would be offensive to the public, holding that Parliament had made it clear that a correct application of this standard should outweigh the right to free expression.

Ofcom also regulates political advertising. Current Ofcom policy is contained in the Advertising Standards Code originally published by the ITC. In effect, advertising on behalf of an organisation whose objects are mainly or wholly political, or advertising which is directed towards a political end, is banned. This covers radio advertising about atrocities in Rwanda and Burundi by Amnesty International. The *Index on Censorship* magazine has suffered a similar ban, which was held not to breach Article 10 of the Convention.

There are limits to Ofcom's duties. The Court of Appeal has accepted that in judging whether all the constituent parts of a programme satisfy the good taste canon, the ITC could take account of the purpose and character of the programme as a whole. The duties set out above had also to be reconciled with ITC's other duties, for instance to secure a wide showing of programmes of merit. Channel 4 was deliberately created to provide programmes calculated to appeal to tastes and interests not generally catered for by ITV, and to encourage innovation and experimentation in the form and content of programmes. Inevitably, this can only be done in some cases at the risk of causing offence to those with mainline tastes. The requirement of impartiality in non-news programmes can be satisfied over a series of programmes and a tradition has developed of allowing more latitude to personal-view programmes that are balanced by others.

The courts have discouraged legal challenges to the ITC and its predecessor, the IBA, for vetting programmes, and their decisions on individual programmes generally can only be quashed if they are so perverse as to be unreasonable. This will undoubtedly also apply to Ofcom.

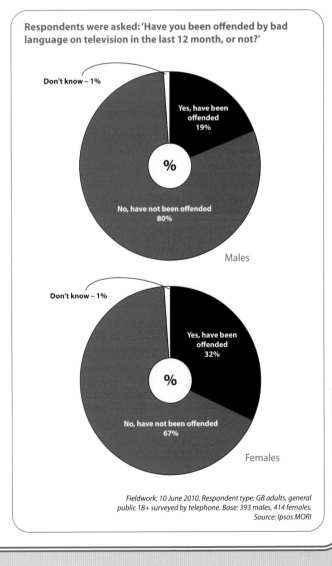

Respondents were asked: 'Have you been offended by bad language on television in the last 12 month, or not?'

Don't know – 1%
Yes, have been offended 19%
%
No, have not been offended 80%
Males

Don't know – 1%
Yes, have been offended 32%
%
No, have not been offended 67%
Females

Fieldwork: 10 June 2010. Respondent type: GB adults, general public 18+ surveyed by telephone. Base: 393 males, 414 females.
Source: Ipsos MORI

YOURRIGHTS

The BBC is now regulated, in part, by Ofcom. BBC compliance with the programme codes is regulated by Ofcom. Issues concerning accuracy and impartiality remain the responsibility of the BBC Governors.

Radio or television programmes broadcast by the independent broadcasters or the BBC can be reviewed by Ofcom. Complaints of unjust or unfair treatment or unwarranted infringements of privacy in, or in connection with, the obtaining of material included in sound or television broadcasts, may be made by a person affected. They are known as 'fairness complaints'. Complaints cannot be made in connection with someone who has died more than five years previously, but within this period a member of the family, a personal representative or someone closely connected can make a fairness complaint to Ofcom. Written complaints can be made by anyone about the portrayal of violence or sexual conduct or about alleged failures of programmes to attain standards of taste and decency – a 'standards complaint' – within two months of a television programme and three weeks of a radio programme.

Ofcom cannot order the payment of any money to the complainant, but can insist on the responsible body publishing Ofcom's findings and, more significantly, can insist on an approved summary being broadcast within a stipulated time.

> *The BBC is now regulated, in part, by Ofcom. BBC compliance with the programme codes is regulated by Ofcom. Issues concerning accuracy and impartiality remain the responsibility of the BBC Governors*

The Obscene Publications Act applies to television and radio broadcasts, although since 1990 no prosecutions have been brought.

⇨ The above information is reprinted with kind permission from YourRights. Visit www.yourrights.org.uk for more information.

© Liberty

Advertising and age

Information from YouGov.

By Rosie Forsyth

While many believe that adverts are misleading, there is a stark contrast between age groups in public demand when it comes to the question of whether advertising regulation should be tightened or not. It seems the older you are, the more likely you are to expect representative, non-misleading advertising.

The Advertising Standards Authority (ASA) is the UK governing body for advertisements, and in its own words, aims to 'keep standards high' and 'ensure advertising stays within the rules' to remain 'legal, decent, honest and truthful'. The ASA reserves the right to remove any advert it deems to have broken its codes and regulations and works largely by investigating consumer complaints.

From our survey, 41% believe that the ASA's current regulatory controls are 'about right', but 22% of those aged 55 and over think that the ASA needs to go 'much further' in tightening controls. In contrast, however, a mere 4% of 18- to 34-year-olds agree. A similar pattern emerges throughout the survey; while 75% think television advertising should 'present the product as accurately as possible', this figure drops to 65% among 18- to 24-year-olds and rises to 82% among the over 55s.

> *41% believe that the Advertising Standards Authority's current regulatory controls are 'about right', but 22% of those aged 55 and over think that the ASA needs to go 'much further' in tightening controls*

It seems younger people are more willing to countenance an advert which 'sells the idea of a product', compared to the older generation who prefer to look to ads that 'present the product as accurately as possible'.

10 June 2010

⇨ The above information is reprinted with kind permission from YouGov. Visit www.yougov.com for more information.

© YouGov

Swearing on television

A new poll published today shows that 73 per cent of people find some swearing on TV offensive.

The poll was commissioned by Mediawatch-UK. ComRes interviewed 1,002 GB adults by telephone between 15 and 17 May 2009. Data were weighted to be representative demographically of all GB adults.

Significantly, the poll also found that 70 per cent believe the regulator, Ofcom, should do more to reduce the amount of swearing on TV. Despite its own communications market research conducted over recent years showing that the majority of people believe there is too much swearing on TV, Ofcom very rarely upholds public complaints on this issue. 60 per cent of people believe that swearing on TV encourages swearing in daily life and 53 per cent believe that children are not effectively protected from swearing on TV.

> *60 per cent of people believe that swearing on TV encourages swearing in daily life and 53 per cent believe that children are not effectively protected from swearing on TV*

Speaking today, John Beyer, director of Mediawatch-UK, said: 'The results of this survey show once again that swearing on TV causes widespread offence and that Ofcom really is not doing enough to allay public concern. We certainly welcome Ofcom's criticism last week of the record-breaking swearing in *Ramsay's Great British Nightmare*, but this action is too little too late.'

Mr Beyer went on: 'Today is also the closing date of our online petition to the Prime Minister which after just six months has attracted more than 5,200 signatures. We are hopeful that Mr Brown, who has expressed personal concern about broadcasting standards, will now directly intervene in this situation and call upon broadcasters and film makers to seriously improve standards of literacy in their media productions.'

Aware of the latest BBC survey, Mr Beyer disputed the finding that people are 'relaxed' about swearing on TV. He said: 'It may be true that swearing "in context" is tolerable but for most people the concern is with swearing that is entirely gratuitous and has no dramatic or any other context whatsoever.

'The BBC should be asking itself how swearing in programmes fulfils its Charter obligation to "sustain citizenship and civil society". Moreover, these findings seem to contradict research carried out by the BBC for *Panorama* in February which found that 55 per cent of people thought there was now too much swearing, while 68 per cent thought language had worsened in the past five years.'

Mr Beyer concluded: 'The time really has come for broadcasters to act on this matter by strengthening the regulations, otherwise they know they risk alienating swathes of viewers. At a time when broadcasting standards matter more and more to viewers and listeners it really is no good pretending that swearing on TV is an issue that can continue to be ignored.'

May 2009

⇨ The above information is reprinted with kind permission from Mediawatch-UK. Visit www.mediawatchuk.org.uk for more information.

© Mediawatch-UK

Obscenity

Obscenity is concerned with the harmful effect of the article on its reader or audience.

The law governing obscene publications is to be found principally in the Obscene Publications Act 1959. Commercial dealings in obscene items, or possession of them for these purposes, are an offence. With or without a prosecution, the items can be seized under a magistrate's warrant and, after a hearing to determine whether they contravene the statute, can be forfeited.

The test of obscenity – to 'deprave or corrupt'

The Obscene Publications Act 1959 adopted as the core of its test of obscenity the famous phrase of Lord Chief Justice Cockburn in 1868: does the article have a tendency to deprave or corrupt the persons who are likely to read, see or hear it?

Courts have since interpreted deprave or corrupt as implying a powerful and corrosive effect. There must be more than an immoral suggestion or persuasion or depiction; it must constitute a serious menace.

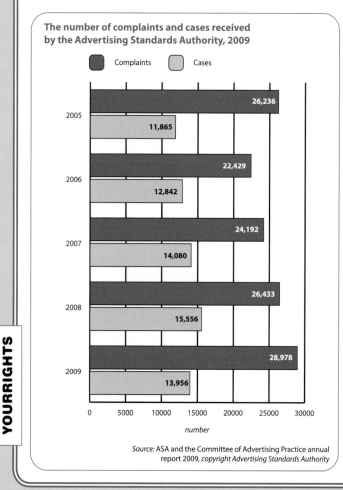

The number of complaints and cases received by the Advertising Standards Authority, 2009

Complaints   Cases

2005 — 26,236 / 11,865
2006 — 22,429 / 12,842
2007 — 24,192 / 14,080
2008 — 26,433 / 15,556
2009 — 28,978 / 13,956

number (0, 5000, 10000, 15000, 20000, 25000, 30000)

Source: ASA and the Committee of Advertising Practice annual report 2009, *copyright Advertising Standards Authority*

The courts must have regard to the effect of the item taken as a whole. What matters is the likely audience, and a publisher is entitled to rely on circumstances of distribution which will restrict those into whose hands the article might fall. It is necessary to show that it would have the tendency to deprave or corrupt a significant proportion of the likely audience.

The law governing obscene publications is to be found principally in the Obscene Publications Act 1959. Commercial dealings in obscene items, or possession of them for these purposes, are an offence

Defence of merit

The most important change introduced by the Obscene Publications Act 1959 was a new defence applying to magazines and books: that publication is in the interests of science, literature, art or learning, or of other matters of general concern. A similar but rather narrower defence applies to plays and films: that publication is in the interests of drama, opera, ballet or any other art, or of literature or learning. The use of this defence was demonstrated in the first major case under the Act when the publishers of D. H. Lawrence's novel *Lady Chatterley's Lover* were acquitted at the Old Bailey in 1960.

Drugs and violence

Obscenity cases do not necessarily involve sex. There have been occasional prosecutions and forfeitures of books that advocated the taking of prohibited drugs. In 1968, while allowing the appeal of the publishers of *Last Exit to Brooklyn*, the Court of Appeal said that the encouragement of brutal violence could come within the test of obscenity. In recent years, 'video nasties' have also been dealt with under the Act.

Indecency offences

In contrast to obscenity, indecency is concerned with material that is offensive to public susceptibilities and is a nuisance rather than harmful. No easy definition

YOURRIGHTS

of indecency exists. The courts have said that this is something that 'offends against the modesty of the average man, offending against recognised standards of propriety at the lower end of the scale'. The standards depend on the circumstances and current standards. This vagueness is problematic. Posters for causes such as animal rights, which are deliberately intended to shock their audience, have sometimes had to contend with indecency prosecutions. Indecency is easier to prove than obscenity because there is no defence of public good, there is no need to consider the article as a whole and there is no need to satisfy the 'deprave and corrupt' test.

There is no general crime of trading in indecent articles as there is with obscene ones, but a number of specific offences incorporate the indecency test. Thus, it is a crime to send indecent matter through the post, or to put it on public display unless entry is restricted to persons over 18 and payment is required, or the display is in a special part of a shop with an appropriate warning notice. The indecency offences do not apply to:

⇨ Television broadcasts; however, the BBC and private television companies operate under internal prohibitions on indecent matter.

⇨ Exhibitions inside art galleries or museums.

⇨ Exhibitions arranged by or in premises occupied by the Crown or local authorities.

⇨ Performances of a play or films in licensed cinemas.

Telephone calls of an obscene nature can also be caught by the indecency laws as a public nuisance. In 1996, the Court of Appeal ruled that a telephone call or calls that cause psychiatric injury can amount to an assault or grievous bodily harm.

In addition to these offences, local councils can now adopt powers to regulate sex shops and sex cinemas in their areas. Council licences always prohibit the public display of indecent material and licences can be revoked if breaches of these conditions occur. Similarly, the music and entertainment licences granted by local authorities will often be conditional on the licensee ensuring that no indecent display takes place. Breach of this condition is both an offence and a ground for withdrawing the licence.

Importation of indecent articles

Customs regulations prohibit the importation of indecent articles. The bookshop 'Gay's the Word' was prosecuted under these provisions for importing books concerned with homosexuality. However, the European Union (EU) provisions on free trade have substantially undermined these restrictions. In the case of the United Kingdom, there is a legitimate market in indecent – but not obscene – articles as long as the traders observe the restrictions noted above. Consequently, Britain cannot discriminate against the importation of the same indecent books from other EU countries. European law prevails over the British customs regulations. For these reasons the prosecution of 'Gay's the Word' was dropped.

⇨ The above information is reprinted with kind permission from YourRights. Visit www.yourrights.org.uk for more information.

© Liberty

YOURRIGHTS

Ofcom says TV channels have 'human right' to broadcast offensive material

Television channels have a 'human right' to show offensive material, according to the industry watchdog.

By Martin Beckford

Ofcom said that its code guarantees freedom of expression to broadcasters as well as the audience's right to view programmes without interference from the authorities.

It made the defence as it rejected a request, made by the mother of two disabled children, to discipline Channel 4 after Vinnie Jones said the word 'retard' on a *Big Brother* off-shoot programme.

The regulator claimed it was 'editorially justified' because the insult was directed at someone who is not disabled, and because viewers of the reality show 'expect a certain level of outspoken banter'.

Lloyd Page, a spokesman for Mencap, the learning disability charity, said: 'As someone with a learning disability, I was disgusted and hurt to hear the word 'retard' used on *Big Brother*. We will never change people's attitudes if this sort of thing carries on. I hope Ofcom will realise why we want this to stop.'

Nicky Clark, who made the complaint, added: 'Channel 4 has a commitment to ensure that diversity is fully and positively represented on its channel. If we are to have our faith restored in Channel 4's suitability to broadcast the Paralympics, it needs to show that it regrets this incident by apologising on air.'

She had complained to Ofcom about an exchange shown on Channel 4's digital channel, E4, during an episode of *Big Brother's Big Mouth* in January this year.

Vinnie Jones was asked how he had known that Davina McCall, the presenter, had entered the *Celebrity Big Brother* house in a chicken costume rather than a fellow contestant.

He replied that it was because she was 'walking like a retard', at which McCall laughed.

Ofcom rejected the complaint that the term was offensive, claiming that the context showed that it was not directed at anyone with any disabilities, and had been used light-heartedly.

Mrs Clark asked Ofcom to review its response but again the watchdog rejected the claim that Channel 4 had breached the Broadcasting Code.

In its second letter, Ofcom wrote: 'Our duties under the Communications Act 2003 require us to take into account such matters as freedom of expression.

'This includes the broadcaster's right "to impart information and ideas" and also the audience's right "to receive information and ideas without interference by public authority" (Article 10 of the European Convention on Human Rights).

'Freedom of expression and the right to broadcast or receive information and ideas will mean that material which has the potential to offend might be transmitted.'

It goes on to say that broadcasters must assure that potentially offensive material is justified by the context of the programme, the time at which it is shown and the expectations of the audience.

Ofcom claimed its own research shows that not all viewers think the word retard is offensive, and that 'many do not see this as an issue'. Mencap says its polls reveal that 61 per cent of Channel 4 viewers do find the word offensive.

The watchdog added: 'We noted the word was directed at Davina McCall and not anyone with learning difficulties. There was not sufficient evidence to conclude that the use of the word was necessarily intended to be offensive to that particular group.'

Ofcom said it was 'unfortunate' that McCall did not 'censure the language' but concluded the 'probable degree of harm and offence was minimal'.

It added that it had twice upheld complaints against broadcasters for using the word retard.

Earlier this week Ofcom ruled that the BBC had breached rules on offensive language when a chef swore under his breath on a mid-morning cookery programme, *Saturday Kitchen Live*.

Channel 4 sent letters to viewers who complained about the use of the word retard, expressing 'regret' that 'in the heat of the moment during a live programme' the insult was 'allowed to go unchecked'.

11 March 2010

Was Mary Whitehouse right about the permissive society?

Information from The Herald.

Yes: Jennifer Cunningham

Mary Whitehouse was a prude who confused respectability with morality. Her fuddy-duddy campaign against portrayals of sex and violence became the symbol of the narrow-mindedness the post-war generation wanted to blow to smithereens. Prominent among them was Joan Bakewell, whose television career included presenting *Taboo*, a series which lived up to the title. A generation on, it is all too clear who won.

The main point of Mary Whitehouse's lifelong crusade was that it was television's 'tide of filth' that was corrupting our children, and that the antidote was censorship

The acceptability of portraying sex on TV has led to ubiquitous images of titillation in adverts, film and the Internet. Details of the sex lives of pop stars and top footballers are known to all through videos on social networking sites and celebrity magazines, lending not just acceptability but the gloss of desirability to behaviour that would once have been genuinely seen as shameful.

To censor, even from the best of motives, is to wield power. Power and corruption are natural bedfellows.

[Whitehouse] had a point. To live permanently at the outer edges is to experience the human condition in as narrow and damaging a way as to be bound by over-rigid rules

To allow the media to portray only 'nice' things, as Whitehouse wanted, is to infantilise society. If a violent rape scene can be censored, for example, how do we guard against particular political views also being deemed unacceptable?

It is no accident that pushing back the boundaries of what could be broadcast, staged or performed coincided with a new openness in which it was possible to shine the light of publicity into dark corners and expose the vile secrets of physical and sexual abuse as crimes. The recognition of the unacceptability of discrimination in any form, now taken for granted, would have taken even longer without the breaking of taboos.

The other side of the coin, however, is the dull, grubby, mindlessness of *Big Brother* and all its reality TV siblings, teenage girls posting pictures of themselves in provocative poses on social networking sites, and sexual acts filmed on mobile phones and displayed on YouTube.

Much of the alarm over the hypersexualisation of society comes from women who, like Whitehouse, are mothers. Parents of young children find themselves thankful for the 9pm watershed which was introduced in the 1964 Television Act largely as a result of her campaigns. Bakewell's sudden acknowledgement that there was more than fear and prejudice behind Whitehouse's warnings that we were on a slippery slope must owe something to concern for her grandchildren.

Whitehouse's approach was wrong: unless each new generation pushes the boundaries set by their elders, we are condemned to stultifying ignorance. But she had a point. To live permanently at the outer edges is to experience the human condition in as narrow and damaging a way as to be bound by over-rigid rules.

THE HERALD

No: Vicky Allan

When it comes to sex and morals, television and the wider media have always been a kneejerk target for a Mary Whitehouse-style wagging finger. If the average age for first intercourse in the UK drops, it must be the fault of 'hypersexualised' TV teen culture. Girls seem to be getting pregnant younger and we assume it must be because of *Big Brother*, or celebrity gossip magazines, or Jordan, or Rhianna, or even skimpily-dressed Barbie dolls.

> *It's easy to blame TV, but our cultural influences are more than just the visual imagery around us. Far more potent are our peers, our parents, and the real world we bump up against*

But isn't this just another case of putting the cart before the horse? Which really came first, the raunch chick or the fertilised teenage egg? The main point of Mary Whitehouse's lifelong crusade was that it was television's 'tide of filth' that was corrupting our children, and that the antidote was censorship.

However, it only takes a quick glance at global figures for teenage pregnancies and age of first intercourse, both litmus tests of the real sexual lives of our young, to realise that it's not quite as simple as that. The Netherlands has the lowest teenage pregnancy rate in Europe, yet it shares roughly the same kind of celebrity-driven, sexualised image culture as our own.

Wander the streets of Amsterdam and you'll meet plenty of Britons who have jetted there to get a flavour of true sex industry liberalism. The Dutch even created that icon of modern voyeurism and permissiveness, *Big Brother*. Sex and pornography-wise it seems that the Netherlands have everything that we have and more, yet they still don't have our teen sex issues.

The average age of first intercourse in Britain is 16 years old: in the Netherlands it is nearly 18 (17.7 years). What then, is the difference, if it isn't censorship? Partly, it's sex education. For the last 20 years the Dutch government has run the 'Long Live Love' programme, one that emphasises the seriousness of sex in relation to consent, the significance of potential pregnancy, and the biological mechanisms behind it. But the country also has a strong culture of parental guidance, which tends to be pragmatic, acknowledging that the young will have sex, but teaching them how to do it responsibly.

It's easy to blame TV, but our cultural influences are more than just the visual imagery around us. Far more potent are our peers, our parents, and the real world we bump up against. The problem surely is that while one element of the permissive revolution – the image culture – took off, backed by the engine of consumerism, the other got left behind. Time for the talk to catch up.

It is time to get serious about sex, not just go Mary Whitehouse and stamp on the X-rating.

6 June 2010

⇨ The above information is reprinted with kind permission from *The Herald*. Visit www.heraldscotland.com for more information.

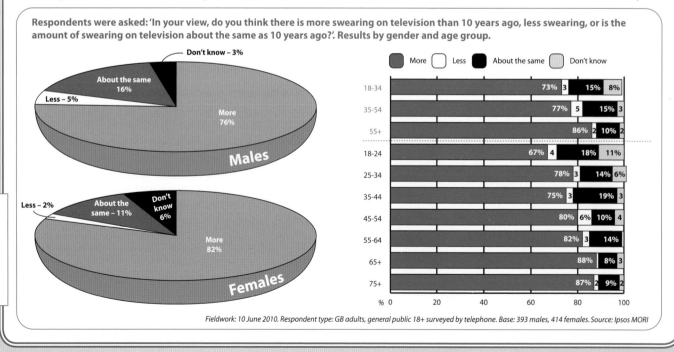

Respondents were asked: 'In your view, do you think there is more swearing on television than 10 years ago, less swearing, or is the amount of swearing on television about the same as 10 years ago?'. Results by gender and age group.

Fieldwork: 10 June 2010. Respondent type: GB adults, general public 18+ surveyed by telephone. Base: 393 males, 414 females. Source: Ipsos MORI

THE HERALD

Clinton warns of 'information curtain'

An 'information curtain' is descending across much of the world, US Secretary of State Hillary Clinton has warned in the wake of Google's revelation of network attacks that originated in China.

By David Meyer

Speaking on Thursday in Washington DC, Clinton said the spread of information networks was 'forming a new nervous system for our planet' and had created an unprecedented number of ways to spread ideas, but that censorship and the use of the Internet to find and penalise dissidents in some countries had seen a 'spike' in the past year.

The Secretary of State's words prompted condemnation from state-controlled newspapers in China, which said the US was trying to impose its cultural values on the rest of the world.

Clinton said electronic barriers to portions of the Internet violated citizens' privacy and contravened the Universal Declaration on Human Rights

On 12 January, Google said its systems and those of dozens more companies had been attacked from within China, resulting in the theft of intellectual property and the attempted hacking of Gmail accounts belonging to Chinese human-rights activists.

The news drew condemnation from the US Government as well as European Commission representatives, who called the attacks a violation of free speech.

'The Berlin Wall symbolised a world divided and it defined an entire era,' Clinton said in her speech at Washington's Newseum on Thursday. 'Today, remnants of that wall sit inside this museum where they belong, and the new iconic infrastructure of our age is the Internet. Instead of division, it stands for connection. But even as networks spread to nations around the globe, virtual walls are cropping up in place of visible walls.'

Clinton pointed out that China, Tunisia and Uzbekistan have stepped up their censorship of the Internet. She said access to social-networking sites had 'suddenly disappeared' in Vietnam, and highlighted the detention last week of 30 bloggers and activists in Egypt.

'Amid this unprecedented surge in connectivity, we must also recognise that these technologies are not an unmitigated blessing,' Clinton said. 'These tools are also being exploited to undermine human progress and political rights.'

Stating that the US supports 'a single Internet where all of humanity has equal access to knowledge and ideas', Clinton said electronic barriers to portions of the Internet violated citizens' privacy and contravened the Universal Declaration on Human Rights.

'With the spread of these restrictive practices, a new information curtain is descending across much of the world,' Clinton said.

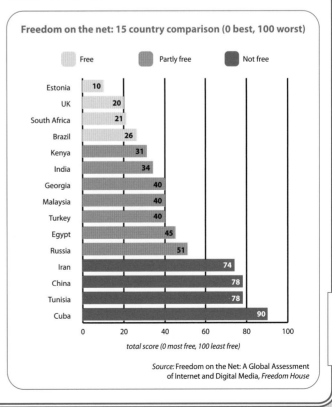

Freedom on the net: 15 country comparison (0 best, 100 worst)

Free   Partly free   Not free

Estonia	10
UK	20
South Africa	21
Brazil	26
Kenya	31
India	34
Georgia	40
Malaysia	40
Turkey	40
Egypt	45
Russia	51
Iran	74
China	78
Tunisia	78
Cuba	90

total score (0 most free, 100 least free)

Source: Freedom on the Net: A Global Assessment of Internet and Digital Media, *Freedom House*

ZDNET

Specifically referring to 'the cyber intrusions that led Google to make its announcement', Clinton repeated her call for the Chinese authorities to conduct a thorough and transparent review of those attacks.

She also urged US media companies to 'take a proactive role in challenging foreign governments' demands for censorship and surveillance'.

'Disguised attempt to impose US values'

China's state-controlled newspapers were quick to respond. The *Global Times*, which is produced by the Chinese Communist Party-controlled *People's Daily*, said in an editorial that Clinton's praise for giving all people equal access to knowledge and ideas 'would be regarded as a new threat' by people outside the West.

'The US campaign for uncensored and free flow of information on an unrestricted Internet is a disguised attempt to impose its values on other cultures in the name of democracy,' the editorial stated.

In her speech, Clinton suggested that 'all societies recognise that free expression has its limits', citing restrictions on hate speech or terrorist recruitment as examples

'The hard fact that Clinton has failed to highlight in her speech is that the bulk of the information flowing from the US and other Western countries is loaded with aggressive rhetoric against those countries that do not follow their lead.'

The paper said unrestricted online access was 'only one-way', because disadvantaged countries cannot produce as much information as Western countries. 'Countries disadvantaged by the unequal and undemocratic information flow have to protect their national interest, and take steps toward this.'

The editorial added: 'The free flow of information is a universal value treasured in all nations, including China, but the US Government's ideological imposition is unacceptable and, for that reason, will not be allowed to succeed.'

In her speech, Clinton suggested that 'all societies recognise that free expression has its limits', citing restrictions on hate speech or terrorist recruitment as examples. Questioned about this statement by an audience member, she said governments should 'err on the side of openness'.

She also urges countries engaging in web censorship to consider the impact of this approach on their own economic growth, arguing that 'if corporate decision makers don't have access to global sources of news and information, investors will have less confidence in their decisions over the long term'.

The Secretary of State also announced plans for the US Government, in conjunction with industry, academia and non-governmental organisations, to create applications and technologies using mobile phones and mapping applications to 'empower citizens and leverage [the US's] traditional diplomacy'.

22 January 2010

⇨ The above information is reprinted with kind permission from ZDNet. Visit www.zdnet.co.uk for more.

Google reveals government censorship requests

**'Government censorship of the web is growing rapidly,'
says search giant as it launches transparency tool.**

By Pete Swabey

Google has launched a tool that allows users to see how many censorship requests each of the world's governments have made to the online search giant.

Between July and December 2009, the UK Government made 59 requests for content to be removed from Google's various sites, most of which related to content on its YouTube video-sharing service, and with 76.3% of which Google 'fully or partially' complied.

The UK's controversial Digital Economy Act, passed into law this month, contains a clause that would allow authorities to restrict public access to websites based on 'any issues of national security raised by the Secretary of State'

This is more than the majority of world governments, but fewer than those of Brazil, Germany, India, the US and South Korea.

Google is unable to reveal how many censorship requests were made by the Chinese Government, whose impositions on the company inspired its recent push towards greater transparency, because that number is itself considered a state secret.

'Government censorship of the web is growing rapidly,' wrote Google's chief legal officer David Drummond yesterday, 'from the outright blocking and filtering of sites, to court orders limiting access to information and legislation forcing companies to self-censor content.'

Drummond wrote that Google believes that providing greater transparency into government censorship will reduce its occurrence.

'We hope this tool will shine some light on the scale and scope of government requests for censorship and data around the globe. We also hope that this is just the first step toward increased transparency about these actions across the technology and communications industries.'

The UK's controversial Digital Economy Act, passed into law this month, contains a clause that would allow authorities to restrict public access to websites based on 'any issues of national security raised by the Secretary of State'.

21 April 2010

⇨ The above information is reprinted with kind permission from Information Age. Visit www. information-age.com for more information on this and other related topics.

The unknown promise of Internet freedom

Information from Project Syndicate.

By Peter Singer

Google has withdrawn from China, arguing that it is no longer willing to design its search engine to block information that the Chinese Government does not wish its citizens to have. In liberal democracies around the world, this decision has generally been greeted with enthusiasm.

But in one of those liberal democracies, Australia, the Government recently said that it would legislate to block access to some websites. The prohibited material includes child pornography, bestiality, incest, graphic 'high impact' images of violence, anything promoting or providing instruction on crime or violence, detailed descriptions of the use of proscribed drugs, and how-to information on suicide by websites supporting the right to die for the terminally or incurably ill.

A readers' poll in the *Sydney Morning Herald* showed 96% opposed to those proposed measures, and only 2% in support. More readers voted in this poll than in any previous poll shown on the newspaper's website, and the result is the most one-sided.

The Internet, like the steam engine, is a technological breakthrough that changed the world. Today, if you have an Internet connection, you have at your fingertips an amount of information previously available only to those with access to the world's greatest libraries – indeed, in most respects what is available through the Internet dwarfs those libraries, and it is incomparably easier to find what you need.

Remarkably, this came about with no central planning, no governing body, and no overall control, other than a system for allocating the names of websites and their addresses. That something so significant could spring up independently of governments and big business led many to believe that the Internet can bring the world a new type of freedom. It is as if an inherently decentralised and individualist technology had realised an anarchist vision that would have seemed utterly utopian if dreamed up by Peter Kropotkin in the nineteenth century. That may be why so many people believe so strongly that the Internet should be left completely unfettered.

Perhaps because Google has been all about making information more widely available, its collaboration with China's official Internet censors has been seen as a deep betrayal. The hope of Internet anarchists was that repressive governments would have only two options: accept the Internet with its limitless possibilities of spreading information, or restrict Internet access to the ruling elite and turn your back on the twenty-first century, as North Korea has done.

Reality is more complex. The Chinese Government was never going to cave in to Google's demand that it abandon Internet censorship. The authorities will no doubt find ways of replacing the services that Google provided – at some cost, and maybe with some loss of efficiency, but the Internet will remain fettered in China.

Nevertheless, the more important point is that Google is no longer lending its imprimatur to political censorship. Predictably, some accuse Google of seeking to impose its own values on a foreign culture. Nonsense. Google is entitled to choose how and with whom it does business. One could just as easily assert that during the period in which Google filtered its results in China, China was imposing its values on Google.

Google's withdrawal is a decision in accordance with its own values. In my view, those values are more defensible than the values that lead to political censorship – and who knows how many Chinese would endorse the value of open access to information, too, if they had the chance?

Even with censorship, the Internet is a force for change. Last month, when the Governor of China's Hubei province threatened a journalist and grabbed her recorder after she asked a question about a local scandal, journalists, lawyers and academics used the Internet to object. A web report critical of the Governor's behaviour stayed up for 18 hours before censors ordered it taken down. By then, however, the news was already widely dispersed.

Likewise, in Cuba, Yoani Sánchez's blog Generation Y has broken barriers that conventional media could not. Although the Cuban Government has blocked access to the website on which the blog is posted, it is available around the world in many languages, and distributed within Cuba on compact discs and flash drives.

The new freedom of expression brought by the Internet goes far beyond politics. People relate to each other in new ways, posing questions about how we should respond to people when all that we know about them is what we have learned through a medium that permits all kinds of anonymity and deception. We discover new things about what people want to do and how they want to connect to each other.

Do you live in an isolated village and have unusual hobbies, special interests, or sexual preferences? You will find someone online with whom to share them. Can't get to a doctor? You can check your symptoms online – but can you be sure that the medical website you are using is reliable?

Technology can be used for good or for bad, and it is too soon to reach a verdict on the Internet. (In the eighteenth century, who could have foreseen that the development of the steam engine would have an impact on Earth's climate?) Even if it does not fulfil the anarchist dream of ending repressive government, we are still only beginning to grasp the extent of what it will do to the way we live.

31 March 2010

⇨ Information from Project Syndicate. Visit www.project-syndicate.org for more.

A censorship model

In comparison to other countries, the UK's Internet censor is starting to look positively trustworthy.

By John Ozimek

Be careful what you wish for, that's the old proverb, and as new and different censorship regimes evolve around the world I begin to wonder whether we Brits haven't been a little harsh on the Internet Watch Foundation (IWF) – our own homegrown attempt to expunge child porn from the Internet.

Over a decade ago, the UK's Internet Service Providers' Association decided that it needed to do something to stem the flow of material featuring the sexual abuse of children. It set up the IWF according to a very simple brief, if it's indecent – and hosted in the UK – report it to the relevant authorities. If it's hosted abroad, add it to a block list. (When this is incorporated into filtering software – routinely applied by almost all UK-based ISP's – access by UK surfers is blocked.)

Lord Carter's *Digital Britain* report praised the IWF and its 'notice and take down' system as being widely regarded internationally as a model. Less than one per cent of child abuse material on the net is now tracked back to this country.

Over the past year or so, other countries have been putting in place their own systems: Romania, Denmark, the Czech Republic and Finland have all joined the blocking club.

In Belgium, and Germany, debate focused on whether judicial oversight should be brought into the process of identifying abusive material. The IWF test is whether it is 'potentially indecent', on the basis of police guidelines. Critics have long argued that this is a recipe for allowing the police to make law.

Both these countries – New Zealand too – toyed with the idea of automatically reporting individuals to the police if they tried to access a blocked URL, despite the fact that such an attempt might be for wholly innocent reasons.

There remains a question of just how accurate a 'secret' list can be – both here and abroad. During the last 12 months, a series of documents leaked to WikiLeaks – has shown that without exception, every single block list has included URLs that simply don't belong on the list: a fork-lift truck company in Denmark; anti-censorship sites in the Czech Republic and Australia. The UK is unlikely to be uniquely free from error in this matter.

Although the UK is apparently alone internationally in opting for the slightly quaint, non-governmental route. In other countries, Internet blocking is established by law and run either by the police (as in Germany) or other bodies associated with censorship (as in Australia). The Carter report notes issues over funding – but doesn't quite grasp the nettle by recommending that the IWF be brought inside the state apparatus.

But is a state-run blocking system really the right way to go? On the question of blocking, while we Brits have politely accepted the existence of the IWF, anti-censorship campaigns in other European countries have focused on just how easy it is to quickly close down abuse sites through the simple expedient of asking ISPs to do so.

In Germany, campaigners proved their point by doing just this: they identified ISPs that were hosting indecent material and tested the system by emailing them with a request to remove it.

Disagreement continues to be the order of the day for more controversial topics – such as adult pornography – but supporters of this approach argue that the taboo on child-based material is so universal that international agreement should be relatively easy.

This obsession with setting up a complex apparatus for blocking or, as in Australia, filtering at source, could be said to raise questions as to whether governmental motives are quite as pure as claimed.

Although there are certainly issues with the IWF approach, ironically, however, just as our model starts to look a little a bit worn around the edges, it may turn out to be rather less threatening – when it comes to civil liberties – than the more 'efficient' models used elsewhere.

2 August 2009

PROJECT SYNDICATE / THE GUARDIAN

Just-in-time blocking

Disabling or attacking critical information assets at key moments in time (for example during elections or public demonstrations) may be the most effective tool in terms of shaping outcomes in cyberspace. Today, computer network attacks, including the use of distributed denial of service attacks, can be easily marshalled and targeted against key sources of information, especially in the developing world where networks and infrastructure tend to be fragile and prone to disruption. The tools used to mount such attacks – called botnets – are now thriving like parasites in peer-to-peer architectures along the invisible underbelly of insecure servers, PCs and social networking platforms. Botnets can be activated by anyone willing to pay a fee, against any target of opportunity.

There are cruder methods of effecting just-in-time blocking as well, like shutting off power to the buildings where servers are located or tampering with domain name registration so that information is not routed properly to its destination. Such just-in-time blocking has been empirically documented by the ONI in Kyrgyzstan, Belarus and Tajikistan and reported in numerous other countries as well.

The attraction of just-in-time blocking is that information is only disabled at key intervals while kept accessible at other times, thus avoiding charges of Internet censorship and allowing for plausible denials of censorship by the perpetrators. In regions where Internet connectivity can be spotty, just-in-time blocking is easily reasoned away as just another technical glitch with the Internet. When such attacks are contracted out to criminal organisations, determining attribution of those responsible is nearly impossible.

Computer network attacks

Just-in-time blocking can take the form of computer network attacks. But the latter can also be employed as a component of military action, low intensity conflict, or attacks on critical infrastructures – in other words, for strategic reasons separate from censorship. For years, such attacks have been speculated upon and it was thought that interdependence among states served as a strong deterrent on their execution. In recent years, however, there have been several high-profile incidences of computer network attacks, including those on Estonia in 2007 and during the Russia-Georgia war of 2008. In each of these cases, the circumstances surrounding the attacks were murky (see 'Patriotic hacking' opposite), but the outcomes were not. In Estonia, key critical information resources, such as 911 systems and hospital networks, were debilitated, as were Georgia's official channels of government communication.

What is most ominous about computer network attacks is that many governments are now openly considering

their use as part of standard military doctrine. President Obama's cyber security review, completed in May 2009, may have unwittingly set off a security dilemma spiral in this respect with its official acknowledgement that the United States has such capabilities at its disposal – a decision that may come back to haunt the information-dependent country when other actors follow suit.

Patriotic hacking

One of the characteristics of cyberspace is that individuals can engage in creative acts that have system-wide effects. This is no less true in cases of individuals taking action against those they consider threats to their own state's national interests. Citizens may bristle at outside interference in their country's internal affairs and can take offence at criticism directed at their own governments, however illegitimate they may appear to outsiders. Some with the technical skills take it upon themselves to attack adversarial sources of information, often leaving provocative messages and warnings in their wake. Such actions make it difficult to determine attribution behind the attacks – is it the Government or the citizens acting alone? Or is it perhaps some combination of the two? Muddying the waters further, some government security services informally encourage or tacitly approve of the actions of patriotic groups.

In China, for example, the Wu Mao Dang, or 50-cent party (so named for the amount of money its members are ostensibly paid for each post made), patrol chatrooms and forums and post information favourable to the regime, while chastising its critics. In Russia, it is widely believed that

security services regularly coax hacker groups to fight for the motherland in cyberspace and may 'seed' instructions for hacking attacks on prominent nationalist websites and forums. A shadowy group known as the Iranian Cyber Army took over Twitter and some key opposition websites towards the end of 2009, defacing the home pages with their own messages. Although no formal connection has been established to the Iranian authorities, the groups responsible for the attacks posted pro-regime messages on the hacked websites and services.

Targeted surveillance/social malware attacks accessing sensitive information about adversaries is one of the most important levers in shaping outcomes, and so it should come as no surprise that great effort has been placed into targeted espionage. The Tom-Skype example is only one of many such next generation methods now becoming common in the cyber ecosystem. Infiltration of adversarial networks through targeted 'social malware' (software designed to infiltrate an unsuspecting user's computer) and drive-by web exploits (websites infected with viruses that target insecure browsers) is exploding throughout the dark underbelly of the Internet. Google's announcement in January 2010 that it had uncovered such a targeted espionage attack on its infrastructure is among the most prominent examples of this type of infiltration.

The growth in this sector can be attributed, in part, to the unintentional practices of civil society and human rights organisations themselves. As our colleagues Nart Villeneuve and Greg Walton have shown, many civil society organisations lack simple training and resources, leaving them vulnerable to even the most basic of Internet attacks. Moreover, because such organisations tend to thrive on awareness raising and advocacy through social networking and email lists, they are often unwittingly compromised as vectors of attacks even by those whose motivations are not political per se. In one particularly egregious example cited by Villeneuve and Walton, the advocacy group Reporters Without Borders unknowingly propagated a link to a malicious website posing as a Facebook petition to release the Tibetan activist Dhondup Wangchen. As with computer network attacks, targeted espionage and social malware attacks are being developed not just by criminal groups and rogue actors, but also at the highest government levels. The US Director of National Intelligence, Dennis Blair, recently remarked that the United States must be 'aggressive' in the cyber domain in terms of 'both protecting our own secrets and stealing those of others'.

Together, these next generation controls present major challenges for monitoring groups, rights organisations, and all of those who care about the future of openness and human rights online. Our own OpenNet Initiative, for example, developed an elaborate methodology primarily oriented towards technically monitoring 'first generation' filtering at key Internet chokepoints using network interrogation tools within countries under investigation. While this mission is still essential and important, its methods are ill equipped to identify the range of next generation controls. To remain relevant, the ONI needs to adjust, perhaps even undertake a paradigm shift, and develop new techniques to monitor more offensive means of blocking. Next generation controls require next generation monitoring.

For rights organisations, darker clouds are looming on the horizon. The context around free expression has become much more ominous and militarised than it was in the past as the norms around next generation controls spread and mature. There is an arms race in cyberspace, with state militaries, extremists, non-state actors and other organisations engaged in increasingly aggressive interventions. Meanwhile, the private actors who control the infrastructure of cyberspace are also becoming more important players in determining the scope for free expression online. Together these present major new challenges and an entirely more hostile context that is becoming the norm. Arms control in cyberspace is now an urgent matter. Lastly, citizens around the world need to be made aware of the threats to the openness of cyberspace that this new generation of controls presents. There is a degradation of valuable global communications occurring as ominous as the degradation of the natural environment. For generations, philosophers have long speculated about a global communications platform through which citizens could communicate, share ideas and develop common solutions to problems in an unmediated fashion. Writing in 1937, HG Wells presented the outlines of such a possibility in his essay entitled *World Brain*:

'The whole human memory can be, and probably in a short time will be, made accessible to every individual … It need not be concentrated in any one single place. It need not be vulnerable as a human head or a human heart is vulnerable. It can be reproduced exactly and fully, in Peru, China, Iceland, Central Africa, or wherever else seems to afford an insurance against danger and interruption. It can have at once the concentration of a craniate animal and the diffused vitality of an amoeba.'

No doubt Wells would shudder if he could see now that having come so close to achieving this very possibility, citizens of the world would allow it to implode in a spiral of weaponisation, militarisation and censorship. A planetary social movement is required today that mobilises us all to protect the net as a forum for free expression, access to information and open communication.

23 March 2010

⇨ The above information is reprinted with kind permission from Index on Censorship. Visit www.indexoncensorship.org for more information.

Censorship, sexuality and the Internet

Information from Association for Progressive Communications (APC).

Put sex and new technology together and you'll always get waves. Victorian societies were scandalised by the arrival of the telephone because women – who were chaperoned at all times – could potentially talk with suitors in private.

Victorian societies were scandalised by the arrival of the telephone because women – who were chaperoned at all times – could potentially talk with suitors in private

Over the last decade, the Internet has been censored and content regulated for a multitude of reasons and the principal reason cited by governments across all geopolitical spectrums has been sex – or 'harmful sexual content'.

What is sexual content on the Internet?

The proliferation of sexual content on the Internet and the considerable size of the pornography market online is a concern to lots of different groups. However, while the online adult sex industry accounts for 12% of web pages, the Internet has also been used to express and explore a range of sexual experiences, relationships and content that cannot be considered 'harmful'.

⇨ Information about sexual health such as breast cancer prevention.

⇨ Information on reproductive health and contraception.

⇨ Sex education for young people, including helping parents and children talk.

⇨ Networks on combatting sexual violence such as the UN's campaign to Say NO – UNiTE to end violence against women.

⇨ Sharing knowledge and information on sexuality and building communities such as by lesbians and transgendered people who meet online in countries where homosexuality is prohibited by law or culture, e.g. Lebanon and South Africa.

⇨ Expressing one's own sexuality on your own terms. In India, online chatting and flirting gives young women a sense of mobility and freedom that doesn't always exist in the offline world where they are restricted in what they wear and who they can talk to.

These are all part of the basket of sexual content on the Internet – and they are all very important to people's right to freedom of expression and right to information. Especially for people who have little access to resources, rights and spaces in the 'offline' world.

What are sexuality and sexual rights?

The concept of sexual rights is built around a positive rather than negative definition. The World Health Organization has a definition of sexuality and sexual rights that were put on paper in UN conferences in Cairo in 1994 and Beijing in 1995. Sexual rights embrace human rights that are already recognised in national laws and international human rights documents. They include:

⇨ personal freedom and autonomy over one's body, sexuality and reproduction;

⇨ sexual relations based on mutual consent and without any form of coercion;

⇨ full respect for bodily integrity;

⇨ respect for and the guarantee of freedom in expressing one's sexual options;

⇨ the recognition of the right to experience a pleasurable sexuality; and

⇨ the existence of the necessary guarantees for the exercise of these rights, including the right to information and user-friendly health services.

Regulation and censorship of 'sexual content'

But scant attention is paid to the types of sexual content mentioned. Instead debates rage on about the moral damage of pornography and the protection of children from Internet paedophiles. And actions in the name of cracking down on 'harmful sexual content' have resulted in:

⇨ banning and blocking of sites by governments – directly or through the encouragement of blacklists.

⇨ censorship of material by Internet service providers (ISPs) – who take down content that goes against their 'terms of use'.

⇨ over-reliance on technical solutions like content filtering by key word – which notoriously fail to distinguish between different types of sexual content, such as those mentioned above.

⇨ technical blunders – leaving swathes of the population unable to use the Internet.

⇨ governments and groups using moral arguments to approve censorship in societies usually proud of their freedom of expression.

These are all different methods of censorship but they have the same impact.

Banning and blocking of sites in the UK

The UK Government relies on voluntary blacklisting by ISPs; however, they only provide Government contracts to those which subscribe to the blacklist. The Internet Watch Foundation which compiles the UK blacklist does not tell websites that they are being blocked and does not make the blacklist public. The IWF 'acts as the morality police for about 95% of UK's Internet users and the fact that one non-government company has so much control over what's decent and what isn't is a bit alarming' (http://www.pcworld.com/article/155156/wikipedia_censorship_sparks_free_speech_debate.html).

Censorship of material by Facebook

Facebook has removed images of women breastfeeding for violating their terms of use referring to content which is 'obscene, pornographic or sexually explicit'. Following one such case, a Facebook protest group was consequently formed and joined by over a quarter of a million people.

Over-reliance on technical solutions like content filtering in the USA and Australia

Despite earlier studies that question the efficacy of filtering technologies to prevent children from accessing harmful content online, or their ability to distinguish between child pornography and other types of sexual content, the Australian Government has proposed mandatory filtering at the ISP level to block hundreds of websites to all Australian Internet users. In the US, a federal law compels schools and libraries that receive federal funding to block sites that appear to default on standards of what is 'acceptable' sexual content.

Government censors site as threat to the image of the Indian woman

In India conservatives see the Internet as a threat to 'Indian culture'. An online adult cartoon strip centring on the sexual adventures of a traditional Indian 'sister-in-law' was banned by the Government. Critics claim the ban was imposed because the site had became so popular – it was more visited than the website of the Indian Stock Exchange.

Brazilian bill proposes draconian censorship

Brazil's 62 million Internet users are guaranteed freedom of expression. However, the Cybercrimes Bill proposed by Senator Eduardo Azeredo to deal with online paedophilia contains such broad and vague provisions that Internet users and bloggers equate it with a draconian media censorship decree that was imposed during the military dictatorship.

New research on sexuality and the Internet from APC

As sexual content and sex-related behaviour online is such a trigger for state and other intervention, APC, the Internet's longest-running progressive online community, is carrying out ground-breaking research on how different people in different parts of the world are really using the Internet related to sex.

⇨ Young women in Mumbai define their sexual rights and what's 'harmful' online;

⇨ How sexuality is at the heart of the Internet regulation debates in Brazil;

⇨ If the content filtering systems in the USA public library systems are really effective or are censoring the information users can access about sexual health and sexuality;

⇨ How the Lebanese gay and lesbian rights movement has grown in tandem with the development of the Internet in the country; and

⇨ How people in South Africa use a transgender community website to find information and support and to 'rehearse' their new identities.

We'll be publishing the results at the end of 2010 but first EroTICs findings are now online.

EroTICs is an exploratory research on sexuality and the Internet carried out by the Association for Progressive Communications (APC) and supported by the Ford Foundation http://www.apc.org/en/projects/erotics

Communications rights that protect sexual rights

Freedom of expression

A fundamental right guaranteed by Article 19 in the Universal Declaration of Human Rights from 1948. It is included in the constitutions of most democratic systems. The International Covenant on Civil and Political Rights (1976) recognises that freedom of expression requires certain restrictions – for respect of the rights or reputations of others and/or to protect national security, public health or morals – but that the restrictions when necessary must be provided by law.

ASSOCIATION FOR PROGRESSIVE COMMUNICATIONS

Freedom of information

The right to freedom of expression is the basis for the right to information. A key aspect of modern democracies is that the ability of citizens to participate in circulating and exchanging information and to communicate in society. As a result society can access diverse opinions and cultural stances. Although national constitutions often guarantee freedom of expression, regulations imposed on media and the Internet do not always allow everyone the same degree of rights to information.

Freedom from surveillance and the right to privacy

Article 12 of the Universal Declaration of Human Rights grants all persons the right to privacy in their lives, families and homes without interference from government or other entities. The Internet's very nature makes personal privacy difficult to ensure but can help people avoid government restrictions. 'Private space' is a very important arena for ensuring people's sexual rights. At the same time, when abuses occur in private spaces, demand for government intervention emerge. So it's a complex right to defend.

Threats to people's sexual rights

Censorship

The use of power by the State or other entity to control the freedom of expression. Censorship is any intent to prohibit access to information, viewpoints or diverse forms of expression.

Content regulation

The ways the free flow of information on the Internet is controlled. Regulation takes many forms and is imposed by different people – governments (e.g. through laws), the private sector (e.g. through 'terms of use' and contractual agreements), the technical community (e.g. through standards and protocols) and individuals (e.g. through installation of filtering software on PCs).

Filtering

Filtering software controls what content a person can see online, filtering the content by key words. When imposed without the user's consent by a government or an Internet service provider this constitutes censorship.

Website blocking

Another form of state or Internet provider censorship, this works by blocking a computer access to a particular Internet address. The user may receive a 'Site not found' message.

April 2010

⇨ The above information is reprinted with kind permission

from the Association for Progressive Communications (APC). Visit www.apc.org for more information.

© *Association for Progressive Communications (APC)*

One in three children under ten have viewed porn online

Information from ParentalControl.

A new study conducted by *Psychologies* magazine has found that one in three kids have seen porn on the Internet before they are ten years old.

Eight in ten children between the ages of 14 and 16 admitted to viewing porn online at home, due to lack of parental controls on the computer or being tech-savvy enough to bypass the restrictions.

However, 70% of British teens report that they haven't been physically intimate with someone, so are viewing explicit and often violent pornographic content well before it comes to the real thing.

Experts warn that this makes individuals more likely to have relationship problems in the future and more worryingly, commit rape.

Sociologist Michael Flood commented, 'There is compelling evidence that pornography has negative effects on individuals and communities. Porn shows sex in unrealistic ways and fails to address intimacy, love, connection or romance. It doesn't mean every young person is going out to rape somebody but it increases the likelihood.'

Two in three teens report that they can easily access porn using the Internet on their mobile phones.

Talking to children about what they look at online is important in helping to protect them. Make sure kids aren't allowed to access the Internet in the privacy of their bedrooms – keep the family computer in a public place where you can check what they are up to. Installing parental control software will also help to block sites with pornographic content, to help protect children online even when your back is turned.

7 June 2010

⇨ The above information is reprinted with kind permission from ParentalControl. Visit www. parentalcontrol.co.uk for more information.

© *Brightfilter Ltd*

700,000 Brits 'still exposed to child abuse'

Information from PCPro.

By Barry Collins

A coalition of children's charities has warned that 700,000 Britons 'can still get uninterrupted and easy access to illegal child abuse images' over the Internet.

Around 95% of Britain's broadband subscribers belong to an ISP that blocks sites based on the blacklist compiled by the Internet Watch Foundation.

However, many smaller ISPs have yet to implement the blacklist, citing high costs and doubts over the effectiveness of the system.

The Children's Charities' Coalition on Internet Safety claims it's time the Government brought the remaining ISPs into line.

'Allowing this loophole helps to feed the appalling trade in images which feature real children being seriously sexually assaulted,' claims Zoe Hilton, policy adviser for the NSPCC.

'We now need decisive action from the Government to ensure the Internet service providers that are still refusing to block this foul material are forced to fall into line. Self-regulation on this issue is obviously failing – and in a seriously damaging way for children.'

Zen Internet says in a statement that it 'has not yet implemented the IWF's recommended system because we have concerns over its effectiveness. Our managing director, Richard Tang, is going to meet Peter Robbins, the Chief Executive of the IWF, to discuss these concerns.'

When pressed by PC Pro on what Zen's exact concerns over the IWF system are, the company declined to comment because Tang was currently on holiday.

The IWF has, however, been at the centre of recent controversy over the ham-fisted way in which ISPs deploy its blacklist.

The watchdog's decision to ban a Wikipedia article on the The Scorpions' *Virgin Killer* album, because it contained a provocatively posed photo of a naked girl, led to millions of British surfers being barred from editing the site.

The furore made the album cover one of the most highly viewed articles on Wikipedia after the ban became public knowledge, forcing the IWF to remove the site from its blacklist.

Similar problems with the web proxies used by ISPs to filter sites on the IWF list led to the Internet Archive being blocked by Demon Internet earlier this month.

'We've now seen two high-traffic sites filtered in the past few months; and on both occasions bad things have happened, which have – rightly or wrongly – brought the IWF into disrepute,' wrote security expert Dr Richard Clayton on his Light Blue Touchpaper blog. 'The underlying policy decisions need reconsideration.'

23 February 2009

⇨ The above information is reprinted with kind permission from PCPro. Visit www.pcpro.co.uk for more.

Pornographic websites	4.2 million (12% of total websites)
Pornographic pages	420 million
Daily pornographic search engine requests	68 million (25% of total search engine requests)
Daily pornographic emails	2.5 billion (8% of total emails)
Internet users who view porn	42.7%
Received unwanted exposure to sexual material	34%
Average daily pornographic emails/user	4.5 per Internet user
Monthly pornographic downloads (peer-to-peer)	1.5 billion (35% of all downloads)
Daily Gnutella 'child pornography' requests	116,000
Websites offering illegal child pornography	100,000
Sexual solicitations of youth made in chat rooms	89%
Youths who received sexual solicitation	1 in 7 (down from 2003 stat of 1 in 3)
Worldwide visitors to pornographic web sites	72 million visitors to pornography, monthly
Internet pornography sales	$4.9 billion

Internet pornography statistics
The amount of pornography on the Internet can be difficult to fathom. A total of 4.2 million websites contain pornography. That is 12 per cent of the total number of websites. There are 100,000 websites that offer pornography and one in seven youths report being solicited for sex on the Internet.

Photo: Brian Lary

Source: TopTenREVIEWS. View these statistics on their website here: http://www.internet-filter-review.toptenreviews.com/internet-pornography-statistics.html

⇨ Governments in China, Russia, Venezuela and other countries have been systematically encroaching on the comparatively free environment of the Internet and new media. Sophisticated techniques are being used to censor and block access to particular types of information. (page 1)

⇨ The world's ten worst-rated countries in terms of press freedom are Belarus, Burma, Cuba, Equatorial Guinea, Eritrea, Iran, Libya, North Korea, Turkmenistan, and Uzbekistan. In these states, independent media are either non-existent or barely able to operate. (page 2)

⇨ 52% of the public want the press regulated by an independent self-regulatory body vs only 8% who want a newspaper industry complaints body – as now. (page 6)

⇨ The foundation of our democracy is the idea that individuals are capable of moral and political reasoning. (page 8)

⇨ Film and video releases in Britain are amongst the most tightly-regulated in the Western world. With only a few exceptions, every commercially-released film both in cinemas and on video will have been vetted by the British Board of Film Classification. (page 13)

⇨ The most significant piece of legislation to affect BBFC classification standards is the Video Recordings Act 1984. This Act requires all 'video works' (films, TV programmes, video games, etc) which are supplied on a disc, tape or any other device capable of storing data electronically to be classified by the BBFC. (page 14)

⇨ On 99% of recent film and DVD viewing occasions, there was agreement with the BBFC classification of films and DVDs seen. (page 15)

⇨ While most video games (50%) are suitable for players of all ages (rated 3), there are many that are only suitable for older children and young teenagers. (page 17)

⇨ Unlike newspapers, which can openly propagate their own views, the television companies cannot editorialise on matters – other than broadcasting issues – which are politically or industrially controversial or relate to current public policy. (page 19)

⇨ 41% of people surveyed believed that the Advertising Standards Authority's current regulatory controls were 'about right', but 22% of those aged 55 and over thought that the ASA needed to go 'much further' in tightening controls. In contrast, however, a mere 4% of 18- to 34-year-olds agreed. (page 20)

⇨ A poll shows that 73 per cent of people find some swearing on TV offensive. (page 21)

⇨ Obscenity cases do not necessarily involve sex. There have been occasional prosecutions and forfeitures of books that advocated the taking of prohibited drugs. (page 22)

⇨ It is a crime to send indecent matter through the post, or to put it on public display unless entry is restricted to persons over 18 and payment is required, or the display is in a special part of a shop with an appropriate warning notice. (page 23)

⇨ Between July and December 2009, the UK government made 59 requests for content to be removed from Google's various sites, most of which related to content on its YouTube video sharing service, and with 76.3% of which Google 'fully or partially' complied. (page 29)

⇨ It is important to emphasise that cyberspace is owned and operated primarily by private companies. The decisions taken by those companies on content controls can be as important as those taken by governments. (page 33)

⇨ Eight in ten children between the ages of 14 and 16 admitted to viewing porn online at home. (page 38)

⇨ 700,000 Britons 'can still get uninterrupted and easy access to illegal child abuse images' over the Internet. (page 39)

The British Board of Film Classification (BBFC)

A body appointed by the government to classify all video and DVD releases.

Censorship

When there are restrictions on what people can see or hear and on the information they are allowed to access, this is called censorship. By censoring something, an individual, publication or Government is preventing the whole truth from coming out or stopping something from being heard or seen at all. Items may also be censored or restricted to protect vulnerable people such as children, and to prevent public offence.

Classifications

Also called age ratings. Films in cinemas and on DVD, as well as computer games, must carry a classification indicating a minimum age at which the material should be watched or played. It is a criminal offence for a retailer to supply an age-restricted DVD or game to someone below the required age.

Defamation, libel and slander

The term 'defamation' refers to false claims made about an individual or group which present them in a negative and inaccurate light. When this takes a temporary form, for example in spoken comments, it is known as slander. When defamatory comments appear in a permanent form – i.e. they are communicated in writing or via a broadcast medium such as television – it is known as libel. Libel is a civil offence and should the person or group libelled wish to do so, they can pursue a claim against the originator of the defamatory comments through the courts.

Freedom of expression

Also called freedom of speech, free speech. This is protected by Article 19 of the Universal Declaration of Human Rights, which states that: 'Everyone has the right to freedom of opinion and expression; this right includes freedom to hold opinions without interference and to seek, receive and impart information and ideas through any media and regardless of frontiers'.

Free press

A free press is one which is not censored or controlled by a government. It allows us to find out what we want to know without restrictions.

The Freedom of Information Act

The Freedom of Information Act states that there should be free access to information about the Government, individuals and businesses.

Gagging order

A ruling which prevents certain information from being made public. For example, if a court case is ongoing, the press can be prevented by law from publishing some of the details if it is felt this would affect the outcome of the case – i.e. by influencing the jury and therefore preventing the defendant from having a fair trial.

Non-violent direct action (NVDA)

Peaceful protesting. This means that an individual can take part in a public protest but it must not involve violence against property or persons.

Press Complaints Commission

The PCC is a regulatory body responsible for ensuring that UK newspapers and magazines adhere to a Code of Practice. The Code aims to ensure responsible journalism by setting down rules on matters such as accuracy in reporting, privacy intrusion and media coverage of vulnerable groups. If a member of the public is affected by unfair media coverage, they can complain to the PCC, citing which part of the Code of Practice they feel has been breached. The Code was laid down by newspaper editors themselves, and the PCC consists of representatives of the major publishers: thus the newspaper industry is self-regulating.

The watershed

The watershed is the name for the 9pm cut-off point in television scheduling, after which television channels can show programmes containing material which may not have been suitable for a younger audience, such as scenes of a sexual nature or swearing.

Additional Resources

Other Issues titles

If you are interested in researching further some of the issues raised in *Censorship Issues,* you may like to read the following titles in the *Issues* series:

⇨ Vol. 179 *Tackling Child Abuse* (ISBN 978 1 86168 503 2)

⇨ Vol. 174 *Selling Sex* (ISBN 978 1 86168 488 2)

⇨ Vol. 168 *Privacy and Surveillance* (ISBN 978 1 86168 472 1)

⇨ Vol. 167 *Our Human Rights* (ISBN 978 1 86168 471 4)

⇨ Vol. 158 *The Internet Revolution* (ISBN 978 1 86168 451 6)

⇨ Vol. 157 *The Problem of Globalisation* (ISBN 978 1 86168 444 8)

⇨ Vol. 153 *Sexual Orientation and Society* (ISBN 978 1 86168 440 0)

⇨ Vol. 148 *Religious Beliefs* (ISBN 978 1 86168 421 9)

⇨ Vol. 142 *Media Issues* (ISBN 978 1 86168 408 0)

⇨ Vol. 134 *Customers and Consumerism* (ISBN 978 1 86168 386 1)

For a complete list of available *Issues* titles, please visit our website: www.independence.co.uk/shop

Useful organisations

You may find the websites of the following organisations useful for further research:

⇨ **Association for Progressive Communications:** www.apc.org

⇨ **British Board of Film Classification:** www.bbfc.co.uk

⇨ **BFI Screenonline:** www.screenonline.org.uk

⇨ **The Free Society:** www.thefreesociety.org

⇨ **Freedom House:** http://freedomhouse.org

⇨ **Index on Censorship:** www.indexoncensorship.org

⇨ **Information Age:** www.information-age.com

⇨ **Media Standards Trust:** www.mediastandardstrust.org

⇨ **Mediawatch-UK:** www.mediawatchuk.org.uk

⇨ **The New Statesman:** www.newstatesman.com

⇨ **Parental Control:** www.parentalcontrol.co.uk

⇨ **PEGI (Pan European Game Information):** www.pegi.info

⇨ **Press Complaints Commission:** www.pcc.org.uk

⇨ **Project Syndicate:** www.project-syndicate.org

⇨ **YourRights:** www.yourrights.org.uk

⇨ **ZDNet:** www.zdnet.co.uk

ACKNOWLEDGEMENTS

The publisher is grateful for permission to reproduce the following material.

While every care has been taken to trace and acknowledge copyright, the publisher tenders its apology for any accidental infringement or where copyright has proved untraceable. The publisher would be pleased to come to a suitable arrangement in any such case with the rightful owner.

Chapter One: The Free Speech Debate

Restrictions on press freedom intensifying, © Freedom House, PCC rejects Jan Moir complaint, © politics.co.uk, What is the PCC?, © Press Complaints Commission, Confusing censoring with censuring, © Guardian News and Media Limited 2010, Who should oversee the journalistic code of practice? [graphs], © Ipsos MORI, Responsibility of newspapers and journalists [graphs], © YouGov, The public and press self-regulation, © Media Standards Trust, PCC attitude survey, © Press Complaints Commission, The BNP: no platform, no exceptions, © LabourList.org, Why 'no platform' is incompatible with freedom of speech, © The Free Society, British troops harassed by anti-war protestors during homecoming parade, © Independence, The Luton protesters should not have been convicted, © New Statesman, Atheists and ASBOs: what price offence?, © Index on Censorship, Press freedom status by country [graph], © Freedom House.

Chapter Two: Regulation and Standards

Censorship and regulation, © BFI Screenonline, Film classification, © BBFC, Film rating symbols and descriptions [diagram], © BBFC, Public opinion and the BBFC guidelines, © BBFC, The age-rating system for video games, © PEGI, Ofcom, © Liberty, Offence from bad language in the last 12 months [graph], © Ipsos MORI, Advertising and age, © YouGov, Swearing on television, © Mediawatch-UK, Obscenity, © Liberty, The number of complaints and cases received by the Advertising Standards Authority, 2009 [graph], © Advertising Standards Authority, Ofcom says TV channels have 'human right' to broadcast offensive material, © Telegraph Media Group Limited 2010, Was Mary Whitehouse right about the permissive society?, © 2010 Herald & Times Group Ltd, Is there more swearing on TV now than 10 years ago? [graphs], © Ipsos MORI.

Chapter Three: Censoring the Internet

Clinton warns of 'information curtain', Copyright 2010 CBS Interactive Limited. All rights reserved. ZDNET is a registered service mark of CBS Interactive Limited, Freedom on the net: 15-country comparison [graph], © Freedom House, Google reveals government censorship requests, © Information Age Media Ltd, The unknown promise of Internet freedom, © Project Syndicate, A censorship model, © Guardian News and Media Limited 2010, Cyber wars, © Index on Censorship, Censorship, sexuality and the Internet, © Association for Progressive Communications, One in three children under ten have viewed porn online, © Brightfilter Ltd, 700,000 Brits 'still exposed to child abuse', © PCPro, Internet pornography statistics [table], © TopTenREVIEWS.

Illustrations

Pages 7, 23, 28, 34: Simon Kneebone; pages 9, 13, 17, 21: Bev Aisbett; pages 10, 18, 25: Don Hatcher; pages 16, 29, 33: Angelo Madrid.

Cover photography

Left: © Bethany Carlson. Centre: © Alen Stojanac. Right: © Armin Hanisch.

Additional acknowledgements

Research by Mark Anslow.

And with thanks to the Independence team: Mary Chapman, Sandra Dennis and Jan Sunderland.

Lisa Firth
Cambridge
September, 2010